CITIES on the REBOUND

A Vision for Urban America

William H. Hudnut III
ULI–the Urban Land Institute

To my wife Beverly and my son Christopher
With whom I live,
Without whom I could not live.

Also by William H. Hudnut III:
Minister/Mayor
The Hudnut Years in Indianapolis 1976–1991

© 1998 by ULI–the Urban Land Institute
1025 Thomas Jefferson Street, N.W.
Suite 500 West
Washington, D.C. 20007-5201

Hudnut, William H., III.
    Cities on the Rebound: A Vision for Urban America.
Washington, D.C.: ULI–the Urban Land Institute, 1998.

ULI Catalog Number: C17
ISBN 0-87420-863-7
Library of Congress Catalog Card Number: 98-87739

Design by Meadows Design Office, Incorporated
Washington, D.C. www.mdomedia.com

Printed in the United States of America.
1 2 3 4 01 00 99 98

CONTENTS

(v) FOREWORD

(ix) INTRODUCTION

(1) CHAPTER ONE:
Creating Positive Change

(13) CHAPTER TWO:
Surfing the Third Wave

(21) CHAPTER THREE:
Partnering for the Common Good

(35) CHAPTER FOUR:
Finding New Neighbors

(59) CHAPTER FIVE:
Minding the Store

(107) CHAPTER SIX:
Creating "Places Worthy of Our Affection"

(155) EPILOGUE

(159) NOTES

(171) INDEX OF SELECTED NAMES AND PLACES

FOREWORD

BILL HUDNUT LIKES CITIES, AND he likes people. He likes to think about what allows cities and people to thrive and what can be done to accomplish that through public policy and individual leadership and action. He does this with a passionate enthusiasm fueled by his four terms as mayor of Indianapolis during that city's emergence as a vibrant city and metropolitan center in the 1970s and 1980s.He also served as president in 1981 of the National League of Cities (NLC).

Bill Hudnut has a point of view that I believe is a priceless asset for a leader, a teacher, or anyone engaged in an effort to influence the thoughts or actions of others, namely, a penchant for the positive. He approaches issues and ideas with a constructive predisposition, focusing on what might be done to accomplish something to benefit the community. Rather than dwelling on the problems or deficiencies at hand, he recognizes their significance and proceeds to look for solutions.

This book is a collection of ideas and suggestions to stimulate community leaders, public officials, employers, consumers, designers, developers, and citizens of all types and outlooks to look at the places where we live and work and to think about ways to make them better: not with bricks and mortar as much as with the attitudes and approaches that go into deciding what to do and how best to go about doing it.

This is a book about vision, leadership, and inclusive collaboration to make our cities and our nation better by building a sense of community and a breadth of stakeholders in that process. It is not about creating uniformity, but about cultivating and harnessing the bounties of diversity. It is about participation and leadership as advocates rather than as adversaries. It is about affirmation rather than defamation. It is about regarding the status quo as a frame of reference that may characterize trends but may not delineate destiny.

"You don't have to be sick to get better" is one of my favorite sayings, and that is the way Bill Hudnut wants us to delve into the ideas he presents about such concepts as smart growth, public architecture, local environmental features, and the relationships among central cities, suburbs, and economic regions. Along the way, he reminds us about attending to tensions involving race and to concerns about public safety, education, jobs, poverty, and housing our social infrastructure as well as the physical infrastructure of transportation systems and other public works. Not a litany of needs or a compendium of solutions, this book is an annotated checklist with some ideas about places and people involved in creative endeavors.

Can cities and their suburbs find ways to build a shared sense of community and to strengthen their combined economic vitality? Can neighborhoods create a climate that celebrates diversity, promotes civic engagement and participation, and nurtures the needs of children and youth, families, senior citizens, newcomers, and others with special needs? Can business leaders, financial institutions, public agencies, nonprofit and philanthropic organizations, civic associations, and religious groups acquire a perspective that allows their activities to blend and harmonize to achieve a greater good for the entire community?

I am convinced that the answer to all of those questions is yes. There are places, people, and projects that can be cited as affirmative examples for some aspect of each question. Bill Hudnut includes many in this volume. They are gleaned from his own extensive experience in Indianapolis, from his many years of involvement with the National League of Cities as a leader and listener, and from his travels, observation, and professional studies while associated with the Hudson Institute, the Kennedy School of Government's Institute of Politics, the Civic Federation in Chicago, and the Urban Land Institute. Other examples abound in work done by NLC and other organizations involved with these issues.

The real test, of course, involves a question that is much more difficult to answer. Will these positive things happen? The desire to do anything cannot, by itself, accomplish the task. Like this book, it can guide and motivate. As in life, it then depends on people, acting individually and collectively, to follow through.

Before seeking public office, Bill Hudnut was an ordained minister from a family with deep roots in the clergy. I believe that background has contributed several valuable qualities to his work as a leader and his ideas as an author. It has made him constantly mindful of what's right for the common good, it has skilled him in matters of patience and persuasion, and it has given him a perspective that extends beyond short-term trends or distractions to keep him focused on the goals and outcomes we should want to achieve.

I share his conviction about the potential for positive change in America, and I commend his ideas as a resource and starting point for work we must all do together.

Donald J. Borut
Executive Director
National League of Cities

INTRODUCTION

DURING THE DARK DAYS OF World War II, our family used to gather around the radio each evening to listen to the news from a Chicago station. I can still hear the famous commentator, Gabriel Heater, opening his broadcast with the words: "There's good news tonight."

Since the end of World War II, many central cities have experienced population loss. Brains and talent have moved out. Jobs and businesses have grown in the suburbs. Cities have lost political clout. They have been hollowed out. All too frequently, downtown buildings and industrial sites have decayed, and the tax base has eroded. Taxes have risen, crime and grime have increased, and inner-ring neighborhoods have deteriorated, as has the quality of education. Urban disinvestment has taken its toll.

But that is not the end of the story. There's good news tonight. Today, America's cities are on the rebound, struggling to be reborn, hurting and healing simultaneously. The urban horizon, often perceived as dark, contains glimmers of light that will, I believe, burst forth in the 21st century.

In this book, I try to craft a vision for the successful city of the future. Having served as the mayor of Indianapolis, our nation's 12th-largest city, for 16 years (from 1976 to 1991), I am deeply concerned about the future of America's cities. My aim is to offer readers a few strategies for getting cities on the road to recovery as we turn the corner into the new century. My intention is to offer guidance rather than definitive answers, suggestions rather than blueprints. I am neither an academic nor a professional researcher. I am a practitioner of the game of politics and the art of "cityship"—that is, partnership with, stewardship of, citizenship in, the city. I have tried to frame a vision for urban America that is shaped by concrete examples from my own experiences in Indianapolis and elsewhere, as well as from my reading and public speaking. For reasons of brevity and focus, some aspects of the urban scene have been omitted—welfare reform and health care, for example, and the legislative battles for tax reform, telecommunications regulation, and funding of unfunded mandates that cities have fought in Washington.

This book is intentionally nonpartisan, for two reasons. First, I learned during the years I was a mayor that there is no Republican or Democratic way to pick up the trash; most municipal officials have similar problems and are exploring common solutions, regardless of partisan affiliation. Second, it will take all parties, all sectors, all citizens working together both to initiate and to realize the changes necessary to save urban America. That's why the metropolitan context is important. Cities do not stand alone. They are part of a larger whole, part of an urban region or "citistate," to use the term coined by two of our seminal thinkers on urban America, Neal Peirce and Curtis Johnson. We cannot talk about the central city without thinking about the suburbs, and vice versa.

For their assistance in the preparation of these pages I would like to thank my colleagues at the Urban Land Institute: Rick Rosan, Rachelle Levitt, Rick Davis, David Mulvihill, and especially Gayle Berens, who spent many hours working on the manuscript with me. I also want to thank editors Nancy Stewart and Eileen Hughes, and graphic designers Betsy VanBuskirk and Meg Batdorff. I am indebted to Neal Peirce, whose writings and friendship have been a source of insight and inspiration to me for many years. Robert Silverman of Atlanta, Charles Kendrick of Boston, John E. Walsh, Jr. of Houston, Robert Engstrom of Minneapolis, and Daniel VanEpp of Las Vegas also offered many useful suggestions. I am grateful to Don Borut, executive director of the National League of Cities, for taking the time to write the foreword. These pages could not have been put together in final form without the thoughtful editing of Micaela Porta and her colleagues at Engine Books, to whom I also express my sincere appreciation.

William H. Hudnut III
ULI–the Urban Land Institute
Washington, D.C.

CREATING POSITIVE CHANGE

THE SUCCESSFUL CITY OF THE FUTURE WILL HAVE
LEADERSHIP THAT ANTICIPATES CHANGE AND
HARNESSES IT TO POSITIVE ADVANTAGE

IF YOU ASK A ROOMFUL of people about the state of urban America, chances are you'll get two responses: first, they will express concern over crime, education, and quality of life issues; second, they will deplore urban sprawl and say they don't want any more development where they live. Most Americans, if prompted, would throw up their hands in despair, shake their heads in resignation, and say that nothing can be done to save our cities from self-destructing. Commuting to work through depressed and decaying urban corridors, steering around potholes, setting out trash that doesn't get picked up, living in fear of crime, worrying about poor instruction in their children's schools, and groaning under ever-escalating tax burdens, Americans may well conclude that nothing in the city seems to be working anymore. Even one of the strongest urban leaders in the country—the dynamic Mayor Ed Rendell of Philadelphia—seems to have succumbed to pessimism after years of laboring mightily to lift his city by its bootstraps and turn it around. In a January 1998 interview, Rendell said, "Forget all the good things I've done. Philadelphia is dying."[1]

However, look in other directions and a different picture might emerge. Many cities are experiencing population increases after decades of decline. Assessed valuations are going up. The line is being held on taxes. Progress is being made in the search for smart growth and sustainable development. Exciting new projects are underway. Citizens are being included in the community's decision-making process. Managers of city operations are striving for greater efficiency. And of course, the economy is booming, creating a rising tide that in recent years has lifted a lot of boats.

The success of our cities—or of any enterprise, for that matter—is possible only with leadership. As we turn the corner into a new millennium, there are encouraging signs that community leaders in the business, professional, academic, governmental, and civic sectors are working to find answers to two key questions: First, how can we get the job done better? And second, what do we need to do next? These are two questions I asked constantly during my tenure as mayor of Indianapolis from 1976 to 1991.

Of course, blight, crime, and grime have been realities in many of our cities for some time, and it is both tempting and easy to conclude that they will continue to be for a long time to come. Such a conclusion discounts the role that leadership can play in revitalizing cities. Building a city is not easy work. It requires visionary leadership, generous commitment, and steadfast use of all available resources. In this book, I will offer my personal vision for the city of the future and provide success stories from across the nation. Today's urban leadership demands extraordinary skills: understanding change, adapting to new technologies, building global and regional alliances, promoting policies that encourage smart growth, luring reinvestment back into the city, thinking positively—rather than fearfully—about the future, assembling collaborative coalitions, and innovating to deal effectively with urban problems of tremendous magnitude. There is no cookie-cutter approach, no magic bullet. What works in one place might not work in another. That is why leadership is an art, not a science; a calling, not a position. Leadership has to be earned—won in the heat of battle.

During the past two years, I have visited some 25 groups of real estate professionals from Atlanta to Los Angeles, Sacramento to Pittsburgh, San Antonio to Salt Lake City. I also have met with a number of mayors and other elected officials at conferences, meetings, and mayors' forums sponsored by the Urban Land Institute. In the course of all these sessions, I have seen signs that responsible leaders in the public, private, and not-for-profit sectors are seriously pondering the future of the communities where they live and work and serve. They are beginning to explore new models for improving the way cities are structured and development occurs. There is an entrepreneurial spirit about them, a willingness to think outside the box, and a desire to disengage themselves from business as usual. French economist J. B. Say coined the word "entrepreneur" at the turn of the 19th century. "The entrepreneur," he wrote, "shifts economic resources out of an area of lower and into an area of higher productivity and greater yield."[2] That is to say, the entrepreneurial spirit is interested in maximizing productivity and doing things more efficiently and effectively. We live in the time of the entrepreneurial American city, when the need for creative, courageous—and enterprising—leaders has never been greater.

The successful city will be led not just by political and business leaders but by a host of concerned citizens who believe in the value of civic involvement. The developer, the planner, the architect; the lawyer, the preacher, the doctor; the banker, the broker, the baker; the seniors, the boomers, and the X-ers will all practice the art of "cityship" that is, the art of city-building. Those who answer the call that went out as long ago as the story of the Tower of Babel—"Come, let us build ourselves a city"— will hold the city in their hearts and hands. They will see themselves as partners in building it up rather than tearing it down, responsible stewards of its resources, constructive citizens who believe in civic involvement, leaders who are willing to take risks in order to create positive change in the communities where they live. It may seem idealistic, in our hard-edged, competitive world, to discuss community building and participation in civic affairs. But there seems to be a growing consensus that this indeed is important. As one architect from Indianapolis put it: "There's so little involvement by architects in community organizations. You just don't see it in our profession. We need to get . . . back to [being] community leaders." That applies to all professions, I think, and especially to the talented individuals in the land use/built-environment business, where men and women make decisions day in and day out that affect the health, safety, welfare, and happiness of communities in this country. The successful city of the future will nurture a cadre of citizen-leaders who recognize the peril to democracy of disengagement and who are prepared to walk a second mile for their community's well-being.

Leadership is an opportunity that comes to many people. Some seize it; others don't. In both the public and private sectors, leaders can emerge from the rank and file if they have a vision, can motivate others to commit to it, and possess the courage and tenacity to see it through. Look at what Mayor Joe Riley has done in Charleston, South Carolina, for example. One of the premier mayors in the nation, he has implemented a vision of urban design that preserves the historic character of his city, making it a very attractive city in which to live and visit. Mayor Richard Daley has taken on the Chicago public school system with substantive reforms in mind. Mayor Brent Coles has preserved the core central city of Boise, Idaho, in the face of northwestern growth and sprawl. Mayor Victor Ashe has made a profound commitment to linking open spaces, greenways, and parks along the riverfront in Knoxville, Tennessee. Mayor Nancy Graham has instilled new vitality and excitement in downtown West Palm Beach, Florida.

In the private sector, too, leaders are creating positive change. At a recent meeting of the Libraries for the Future organization, those who attended heard about the work of Peggy Dye in New York City's Harlem. Dye was staffing a voter registration booth one hot day when she decided to take a break. Stopping in at the George Bruce Library and hearing that it might be closed for lack of funding, she took up the cudgels of public advocacy to "stir up spirit," as she put it, and ultimately rallied enough support to convince the downtown "powers that be" to keep the library open. Dye understood how the library and the community are connected. In preserving the library, she and her cohorts saved not only a community information resource and a place of learning and self-education but also a free, accessible public space to which children could repair for safe haven and where newcomers could acculturate themselves in a new country.[3]

Then there is Joe Canizaro, a successful businessman and civic leader in New Orleans. Canizaro frequently talks about "making a visible difference." He once told an audience of real estate developers: "We can no longer measure the success of our cities by office occupancy rates. It will take leadership, vision, clearly articulated goals and strategies, and a determined commitment to make our cities work. Ultimately, it's up to you and me—working within an enlightened business community—to lead the way." But Joe doesn't just talk; he acts. Concerned about the deterioration of the Lower Garden District adjacent to New Orleans's downtown, and worried that this blight might destroy confidence in and the value of downtown properties, he assembled a board of directors, the Community Resource Partnership. Working with local government, residents of the District, and the business community, the Partnership brought common and vested interests together, enacting a master plan for the revitalization of 1,500 units of low-income housing. Now the old units are being demolished, to be replaced by new units occupied by residents with a mix of incomes. Says Canizaro: "We have to have a quality urban core, or business will leave and tourists won't come. This is one small part of it, but a part worth fighting for."

Embracing Change

The ancient Greek philosopher Heraclitus posited, "There is nothing permanent except change." Some 2,500 years later, President John F. Kennedy observed, "Change is the law of life. And those who look only to the past or the present are certain to miss the future." How will we respond to the challenges of colossal change in all aspects of life? How should cities harness change so that they catch, not miss, the future?

We live in a time of rapid change. The challenge is to make change our friend, not our enemy. In his brilliant 1961 book, *The City in History*, Lewis Mumford refers to the city in terms drawn from biology and ecology. The city is an organism. It can decay or grow, disintegrate or progress, die or be reborn. He points out that in every organism, the anabolic and the catabolic processes—the constructive and the destructive—are constantly at work, suggesting that the life and growth of cities depend not on the absence of negative conditions but on a sufficient degree of equilibrium and a sufficient surplus of constructive energy to permit continued repair.[4]

Technological Change

We live in the postindustrial era; the smokestack has been replaced by the computer. The information age is fast upon us, and success will belong to those who enjoy information dominance. Computers and information technology are changing our lives to an extent we could not have foreseen just a few years ago, linking people and ideas across great distances. More than 57 million people in the United States now have access to the Web. It's been estimated that as of early 1997 there already were 650,000 Web sites on the Internet. The new engines of economic growth are being driven by semiconductors. Canadian economist Nuala Beck reports that at present 72 percent of America's gross domestic product is attributable to knowledge-based industries. The world is growing smaller as goods and knowledge travel faster. Old jobs, mostly unskilled and semiskilled, are being eliminated; new, more sophisticated ones are being created. Microchips are doubling in density and speed every 18 months. Computers and robotics are doing jobs in design and production that people once did. New forms of electronic infrastructure are emerging; work sites are becoming more dispersed. Deteriorating physical infrastructure is being rebuilt; buildings are becoming "smarter."

We are surrounded by technological change.

Economic Change

We operate in a global economy; the world is our neighbor. Huge corporate mergers are taking place. New ways of valuing information-age assets are coming into being. Financial markets have been globalized, and foreign trade competition has intensified as multinational corporations have proliferated. Notwithstanding the recent setbacks there, Asia, with its burgeoning and increasingly literate population, will continue to be a major catalyst of global growth.

To stay competitive, business and government will have to become more entrepreneurial, and the workforce will have to be better educated and more appropriately trained. Downsizing and rightsizing are strategies common in most boardrooms. Demassification is occurring with the development of more custom-tailored services and products that offer consumers broader variety and higher quality. The range of choices available to average citizens is nearly dizzying, and more people have the disposable income to enjoy them.

We are surrounded by economic change.

Environmental Change

While world food production has increased dramatically since 1950, famine still ravages millions of people each year. The burning of fossil fuels has led to global warming. Deforestation is accelerating. Lakes and streams have been acidified. Habitats and ecosystems have been destroyed for the sake of sprawling development. Toxic waste dumped willy-nilly into the ground for generations is coming back to haunt us, and the cleanup of brownfields (parcels of abandoned or contaminated land) has become a monumental task. Indoor pollution is causing growing concern: People now worry about whether their homes are contaminated with radon, asbestos, lead, and bacteria from air-handling systems.

It's encouraging to see that increasing numbers of responsible individuals and groups now recognize environmental causes as central to the well-being of our country. They are determined to combat pollution; reduce and recycle solid waste; reclaim land stripped by mining and other forms of development; protect coastlines and endangered species; develop nonfossil fuels; and preserve green space, open space, wetlands, and wildlife refuges. Heightened eco-awareness is becoming evident in a patchwork of initiatives, some of them no doubt impelled by grass-roots political clout. For example, taking the sustainable approach, the local government in Mentor, Ohio, spent more than $9 million to preserve some 450 environmentally sensitive woodland acres from intensive residential development, favoring the long-term benefits of biodiversity over the short-term windfall of real estate profits.

We are surrounded by environmental change.

Social Change

As we move into the 21st century, we will witness a tremendous increase in the elderly population and a massive migration toward the sunshine. By 2020, women will account for about the same percentage of the workforce as men. The white share of the labor force will decline from 76 percent today to 68 percent by 2020. The African-American share will remain at about 11 percent, while the Asian and Hispanic shares will grow to 6 and 14 percent, respectively. The workforce will be divided among those who are proficient in math, science, and languages, and therefore command generous compensation; those who have low-skill jobs and commensurately low incomes; and those who have very little education, no technological or vocational experience and, often, no employment.[5] Meanwhile, social problems like homelessness, AIDS, and drug abuse will require continued attention.

Every major city is divided between the haves and the have-nots. For the most part, those who can afford it are pursuing the American dream in the suburbs. The emerging urban form is characterized by so-called suburban urbanization and the rise of urban villages (concentrations of jobs and markets in the suburbs) or edge cities that offer low-cost land, access to highways, regional-scale shopping, extensive office space, easy parking, hotels and restaurants, urban entertainment centers, multifamily housing, and a short commute by car to high-income suburban housing—in short, new downtowns in suburbia.[6] At the same time, a backlash against growth is occurring as traffic congestion increases; crime moves to the suburbs; and transportation, water, and sewer infrastructures are stretched beyond capacity.

We are surrounded by social change.

Political Change

The Reagan revolution began a process of devolution of power and authority to state and local government as a way of limiting the growth of big government at the federal level, but that initiative is now fading. While the movement was not particularly effective, it did lead to efforts to make government more efficient and entrepreneurial.

Today, new forms of governance are taking shape. Relationships among governmental jurisdictions are mutating. "Reinventing" government has paralleled private-sector initiatives to reengineer and restructure service delivery systems and methodologies. Regional cooperation is seen as a new imperative, as is a more inclusive approach to decision making. The demographic decentralization that we have experienced as a nation has engendered more debate about public policies relating to growth and the revitalization of central cities. Homelessness has dramatized the need for more affordable low-income housing.

New forms of campaigning and voting are emerging: Those who used to campaign door to door in political races are now phoning or mailing letters to raise escalating sums of money and are campaigning via the Internet and TV screens. Voters no longer vote straight tickets or in blocs but instead follow more complex patterns dictated by fragmented interests.

We are surrounded by political change.

Whether we look at these transformations in the way we live and work as bane or boon, they are a fact of life, and we must deal with them. It is said that the Chinese word for crisis is also the word for opportunity. These changes challenge cities to reinvent the way they do business. They offer opportunities to rethink missions, restructure systems, and reengineer operations. Wayne Gretzky, the famous hockey player, once said that while most players skate to where the puck is, "I skate to where it's going to be." Where do people who care about the city want to go from here, with all this change awash on their doorstep? How should cities respond to the challenges of the future? Ask always: What do we do next?

Vision or Perish

"Where there is no vision, the people perish." Proverbs 29:18

There can be no vision without imagination. This is the first step— think creatively, stay open to a wide spectrum of possibilities, and keep it relevant. A vision cannot be put together carelessly. To succeed, it will demand thoughtful consideration and painstaking care. Then it has to be communicated with enthusiasm and clarity. Otherwise, how will others be moved to share it? Finally, the dream has to be cultivated with courage and perseverance, for it will not be easy to realize.

In Indianapolis, at the beginning of my 16 years as mayor, I assembled a small group of community leaders who invested considerable time in a "visioning" process, trying to figure out where we wanted to be heading as a community. One of the dreams we thought worth pursuing was that of becoming the amateur sports capital of the country. From our discussions there grew a realization that we had to build on the strengths we had, such as a central geographic location; a strong commitment to health and wholeness of body, mind, and spirit (represented by Eli Lilly and Co., the Indiana University School of Medicine, and Purdue University); and a keen interest in sports.

From that point, we drew the conclusion that perhaps we could use athletics to improve our city's economy, job base, image, and civic spirit. (In 1984, *Urban Land* magazine described our strategy as "leveraging amenity infrastructure.")

When it came time to communicate this vision to others, we formed a speakers' bureau to get the word out to neighborhoods, civic organizations, various constituencies—and not last or least, government officials. We met privately with a number of state legislators and city council members (always within the framework of our state's sunshine laws, I might add, violating none of the open meeting laws for public officials), and we put our case to media leadership. Our aim was to motivate others so that they would believe in our dream and support it.

Then we had to cultivate the vision, which is to say, make it happen. We raised money. We built sports facilities, to the tune of about $160 million. We dealt with lawsuits. We sought to attract national governing bodies—like the Track and Field Congress and the U. S. Gymnastics Federation—to our city. We tried to expand our outreach into the sports medicine field. We set up an Indiana Sports Corporation to concentrate on holding large-scale events, like the 1987 Pan Am Games.

The result? Indianapolis was no longer known as "Naptown" or a "brick-yard in a cornfield." *Newsweek* called us the "Cinderella of the Rustbelt." The *Wall Street Journal* dubbed Indianapolis "Star of the Snowbelt." A Detroit news-paper wrote something on the order of "Indianapolis is awake year-round now." After the Baltimore Colts moved to Indianapolis in 1984, *Time* magazine proclaimed "India-no-place no more." Gradually we became a very competi-tive city, owing it all to a vision we created, communicated, and cultivated.

As we ponder the changes that are swirling around us, and as we ex-plore their implications for our vision of the successful city of the future, it strikes me that six crucial challenges face us. It is my belief that the future of the 21st-century city depends on the ability or failure of public, private, and not-for-profit leadership to meet these challenges.

I envision a successful city/region of the future offering its citizens a good quality of life and a competitive edge in our world economy. This can be accomplished if the city or region meets the following requirements:

- Has vigorous, visionary civic and political leadership that practices city-ship (citizenship in, stewardship of, partnership with, leadership for, the city);
- Understands and accommodates itself to the transition to a postindustrial era;
- Collaborates, includes rather than excludes, and embraces diversity as a core strength;
- Thinks and acts globally, regionally, and locally;
- Delivers services efficiently and copes effectively with such urban problems as crime, education, housing, transportation, infrastructure, and environmental degradation;
- Limits "bad" sprawl, has a vibrant central city, and promotes smart growth.

Just as Mumford claims, cities are organisms that are always in flux. If their leadership can find keys to unlocking a more creative understanding of what the future will require, they may escape the backwater of history. Futurists Alvin and Heidi Toffler conclude their recent book, *Creating a New Civilization*, by reminding us that "the responsibility for change . . . lies with us. . . . We have a destiny to create."[7] Certainly, where there is no gumption—much less vision—cities perish. We can continue to accept passively communities that fail to sustain us, or we can demand, preserve, and build the kinds of places we truthfully wish to call home. "Either way, that choice is up to us."[8]

THE SUCCESSFUL CITY OF THE FUTURE WILL HAVE VIGOROUS
VISIONARY LEADERSHIP IN ITS PUBLIC AND PRIVATE SECTORS.
THAT IS PART ONE OF MY VISION.

SURFING THE THIRD WAVE

THE SUCCESSFUL CITY OF THE FUTURE WILL
EMBRACE THE POSTINDUSTRIAL ERA

WHILE MANUFACTURING WILL ALWAYS BE important, its role in the economy seems to be diminishing as that of information technology increases, just as the role of horse-drawn plows and carriages became obsolete with the advent of the steam engine and electricity. The marriage of telecommunications and computers in the postindustrial era has made knowledge the new capital. In our fast-paced, "Third-Wave" global economy, information equals power. This became clear during the Gulf War, when industrial-age antiaircraft systems were rendered impotent by Third Wave stealth aircraft. The Tofflers, who coined the Third Wave phrase, conclude: "The globally competitive race will be won by the countries that complete their Third Wave transformation with the least amount of domestic dislocation and unrest."[1]

Make Way for Knowledge

What does this mean for cities? They should surf the Third Wave by courting and playing host to knowledge work, for this will help to create jobs and to broaden the tax base. They should maximize opportunities for employment in that sector—from biotechnology startups and high-flying computer and electronics firms to data-drenched services from the worlds of finance, accounting, consulting, education, medicine, and communications to information-driven transportation and manufacturing. In tandem with the growth of job opportunities, cities must establish training and development programs for young people and those seeking to acquire new skills to enhance or change careers. As Reid Ewing, associate professor at Florida International University, has written, "The economic winners are cities that have made the transition from industrial economies to advanced service economies or have piggybacked on high-tech industrial growth within their regions."[2] Little wonder, then, that a group of Los Angeles real estate professionals included in their 1998 conference on trends facing their industry a panel called "Technology: Real Estate's Newest Partner."

Silicon Valley is perhaps the most prominent example of a place that owes its remarkable growth to high-tech industry, but there are many others. On the drive into Washington, D.C., from Dulles Airport, one marvels at the proliferation of high-tech and telecommunications firms; drive in from Maryland, and a sign tells you you're on the I-270 Technology Corridor. In Columbus, Ohio, Mayor Greg Lashutka created a task force to review his city's role in technology and the future. Among nine recommendations of the task force: expand Ohio State University's science and technology campus and the Edison Program's Business Technology Center, encourage academic support of business, establish a venture-capital pool and advisory network, develop technology-friendly tax codes, and support public-access technology centers.[3] In Staten Island, the Port Authority of New York and New Jersey invested $70 million to develop infrastructure for a new, high-tech office park. Construction of this teleport has resulted in 2,100 new jobs in five fully leased buildings in such industries as computer operations, communications, security, building services, back-office functions, and telecommunications. Merrill Lynch built its worldwide data center there, and Telehouse, a Japanese company partly owned by AT&T, also built a facility to house and operate mainframe computers and telephone switches for customers. Experts say that there may be as many as 200 such teleports—broadband hubs providing users with shared access to high-speed telecommunications and other services throughout the world—by the year 2005.[4] And then, of course, there's Seattle and Microsoft.

Another implication of the technological revolution is that successful cities will harness new methodologies to serve the public more efficiently and effectively. Cities like Indianapolis are now working on the development of a long-range comprehensive technology master plan, asking themselves such questions as: Why make people come downtown to get a marriage license or a dog tag? Why not let them do it from a kiosk in a shopping mall? How can we cut down on paperwork and speed up a city-services delivery system?

Consequently, electronic city halls are springing up all over. The National League of Cities reports "widespread successful city-led efforts" in this area, defining "widespread" as an astounding 79 percent.[5] Many cities, like Boulder, Colorado; Santa Monica, California; and Virginia Beach, Virginia, have public electronic networks that post useful civic information—city council meeting schedules, employment opportunities, public school addresses and phone numbers, a municipal services directory—that is readily accessible by the public. Is it possible that the information-age economy can breathe new life into our cities, despite the decentralization and deurbanization that are resulting from that same economy? Do the cities not contain deep reservoirs of telecommunications, information technologies, universities, cultural institutions, highly skilled workers, and investors who provide a milieu in which knowledge-based industries can thrive? According to *Business Week*, cities are no longer forgotten islands but emerging centers of commerce in knowledge and entertainment: "The durability of cities' key role in the information economy is crucial. If urban areas flourish, they create powerful, efficient engines of growth."[6] In short, the postindustrial era need not consign central cities to the dustbin of history. Instead, it can provide them with new opportunities for growth and renewal.

The Need to Stay Connected

Paradoxically, while the technological miracles that we are witnessing are shrinking the world, they also are making the distance between people greater. "Turn on, tune in, drop out" was the motto of the 1960s, but it works just as well in cyberspace. Obviously, technology is bringing people together—through E-mail and chat rooms, virtual offices and classrooms—but it's doing so electronically, not personally. David Shenk, author of *Data Smog: Surviving the Information Glut*, has written that today's specialization fuels progress while also creating isolation. "Because of demassification, we collectively know more but share much less with the community writ large."[7] Connecting people electronically can disconnect them socially, psychologically, and emotionally. Consider electronic voting in Congress. Congresspersons run to the floor to vote, stick their cards in computer terminals, register their decision, and then run back to their offices and cubicles. It's not hard to see how such an absence of teamwork could lead to a less civil, more ego-driven, hostile environment. Paul Goldberger, former architecture critic of the *New York Times*, says that technology is "fine tuning our commonality out of existence." Like suburbanization, technology isolates us, detaches us, disengages us from downtown and urban values. So does corporate mobility, the culture's emphasis on instant gratification, and the demassification that is making everything small, focused, niched, and segmented (like chat rooms). Goldberger suggests that cyberspace is a tool, not a place, and that people who value separateness (sitting at home staring at the screen of a TV, PC, or laptop) over togetherness, will contribute to the disintegration of American society. "Hold onto the public realm," he pleads. "Don't lose common ground. Stay in touch . . . personally and collectively."[8]

Herein lies a real challenge for business and development professionals, neighborhood organizations, faith-based institutions, and public officials: to create a genuine community. Human nature most often requires linkages and interactions between people as a precondition for creative work (the artist who works alone is an exception). In *Grassroots Leaders for a New Economy*, Douglas Henton et al. explore the implications of the postindustrial economy for community and make the telling point that electronic communications, while important, are no substitute for "face-to-face exchange within teams, where people live and work in close proximity . . . [or] for the trust, sharing, and intense interpersonal interaction essential for the creative process."[9] The heart and soul of the new economy—where the action is—will be tied to place, they observe. And when you talk place, writes Neal Peirce, the noted urban journalist, "you talk town and city—places with restaurants, cafés, walkable streets, shared meeting spaces . . . walkable town centers and neighborhoods . . . easier access to transit and a mix of housing and shops and civic facilities." Peirce and Henton believe, as Peirce puts it, that corporations "large and small, seeking efficiency, competing for knowledge workers, will seek out those towns, cities, and citistate regions that offer beckoning, vital centers, learning environments, and friendly pedestrian environments."[10] Successful cities of the future, take note! "Cityship" looks for space that encourages face-to-face relationships.

The successful city of the future will help people connect. It will promote community-building initiatives and create opportunities and places for folks to socialize: parks, arts and cultural programming, continuing education facilities, greenways, open spaces, festival marketplaces, libraries, town hall meetings, churches, lodges, restaurants, and cafés. Living in this age of high tech/low touch has made us hungry for interaction. How else can one explain the wild success of urban entertainment destinations?

Urban Entertainment Districts

Entertainment is being recognized as a key component in such real estate developments as urban entertainment districts (UEDs)—large-scale urban redevelopment projects, shopping centers, residential towers, cultural facilities, and resorts. UEDs are leisure destinations where sports, shopping, culture, entertainment, and nightlife are frequently encompassed in one development or district.

Operators of suburban malls are conscious of the need to provide places and opportunities for people to congregate. For the most part, though, UEDs will be found in the heart of urban centers, where they are functioning as catalysts for urban revitalization. In this context, entertainment is used as an anchor or magnet to enhance retail, hospitality, residential, or mixed-use development. UEDs do not represent a fin-de-siécle fad, but rather "the nascent reemergence of America's downtowns and commercial districts as major entertainment centers."[11] The long-term result of this trend might well be the transformation of the central business district into the central social district.

Consequently, the successful city of the future will understand the role that UEDs can play in urban revitalization. MCI Center, a 1.05 million-square-foot, state-of-the-art sports arena in downtown Washington, D.C., provides a home for the NBA Wizards, the WNBA Mystics, the Washington Capitals hockey team, and the Georgetown Hoyas. It has 20,000 seats and 110 luxury suites. The facility also has a significant entertainment component that includes a 30,000-square-foot Discovery Channel Destination store, a Discovery Channel Theater, the Velocity Grill, the National Sport Gallery, and a sports team store. The project has brought an estimated $100 million-plus in new business and resultant tax income to the District of Columbia, and it has provided the impetus for the creation of the first business improvement district (BID) in the capital. In Indianapolis, when we added an $80 million domed stadium to the convention center in the early 1980s and brought the Colts from Baltimore in 1984, an immediate $15 million investment in street improvements was made. The money spent up front came back manyfold in the form of a 384 percent increase in tourism by the end of the decade. In the rebuilding of historic downtown Kansas City, 12 city blocks are being set aside for a UED known as the Power and Light District. This $454 million project, aimed at revitalizing 30 acres of blighted property in the heart of the city, has been approved by the voters. If all goes as planned, when this ambitious development is completed at the dawn of the new century, it will feature a 30-screen movie megaplex, traditional and themed restaurants (including a Planet Hollywood), entertainment venues, housing, lodging, offices, and retail. The goal is to create a unique downtown place consonant with the culture and values of this great midwestern city that will attract suburbanites as well as city dwellers. "This is the next iteration of downtown development," states managing director Nick Bashkiroff.[12]

UEDs expand a city's tax base by attracting more residents, shoppers, and visitors, and more jobs, activity, and vitality to the downtown area. Coupled with traditional development patterns in urban housing, retailing, culture, hotels, and restaurants, UEDs add to downtown's image by bringing the "sparkle" that makes other components work.

UEDs have been difficult to finance, however. Urban land is expensive to assemble, infrastructure has to be put in place, construction and operating costs are high, and zoning may have to be changed. This means that a city will have to participate in the project through some form of gap financing: writing down the cost of land, offering abatements or other tax incentives, equity partnerships, grants, or industrial revenue bonds; also, perhaps, offering extra security, infrastructure modifications, zoning variances. Although they are hard to get off the ground, the UEDs generate benefits that make perseverance worthwhile. Cities that ignore this new trend will be the poorer for it.

To be successful, downtowns will need to find ways to connect people in diverse settings. The current widespread construction of professional sports arenas may level off or decline within a few years, but these stadiums, located downtown, help to hold the central core. Why else would Detroit be building a new ballpark downtown for its NFL team, the Lions, and saying goodbye to the Silverdome, located far out in Pontiac, Michigan? Entertainment districts, casinos, convention centers, waterfront destinations, urban malls, athletic facilities, and cultural venues act as magnets that pull people back into the city from the isolation in which they find themselves. So do good transit systems, government and institutional complexes (such as universities and hospitals), a healthy dose of commercial and retail development, and revitalized housing.[13] In all these ways, good cityship helps people to fulfill their gregarious instincts and interact in this day of technologically induced detachment.

THE SUCCESSFUL CITY OF THE FUTURE WILL WELCOME THE INFORMATION AGE WHILE PROVIDING WAYS FOR PEOPLE TO COME TOGETHER. THAT IS THE SECOND PART OF MY VISION.

PARTNERING FOR THE COMMON GOOD

THE SUCCESSFUL CITY OF THE FUTURE WILL
PRACTICE COLLABORATION

"THE NEW MODEL OF LEADERSHIP is collaborative, requiring widespread participation and collective decision-making," suggests the Eisenhower Leadership Group at the University of Maryland in their 1996 report, *Democracy at Risk*.[1] This model keeps faith with the ancient civic virtue practiced by the likes of Cicero, who defined the commonwealth as a "partnership for the common good." Collaborative leadership, which values cooperation over partisanship and civility over disrespect, will characterize the 21st-century city. The era of white male dominance must end. All citizens need and should have the opportunity to participate in the democratic process.

Toward a "Healthy, Robust Civic Sector"

In a successful city, people will not always be squaring off against each other but will work together, as Cicero suggested, for the common good. Leaders of all stripes will practice the art of cityship, addressing tough issues with candor and relating to one another with respect. Such a collaborative effort can establish a standard of behavior that permeates both the public and private realms, preparing the cultural soil for a civil society to take root.

"Civil society," as described by former New Jersey Senator Bill Bradley in a speech before the National Press Club, "is the place where Americans make their home, sustain their marriages, raise their families, hang out with their friends, meet their neighbors, educate their children, worship their god. It is in the churches, schools, fraternities, community centers, labor unions, synagogues, sports leagues, PTAs, libraries, and barber shops.

It is where opinions are expressed and refined, where views are exchanged and agreements made, where a sense of common purpose and consensus is forged."

It is a place, Bradley continued, that "lies apart from the realms of the market and the government and possesses a different ethic. The market is governed by the logic of economic self-interest, while government is the domain of laws with all their coercive authority. Civil society, on the other hand, is the sphere of our most basic humanity—the personal, everyday realm that is governed by values such as responsibility, trust, fraternity, solidarity, and love."[2]

Bradley is suggesting that democracy works best when public-spirited citizens collaborate in the actual work of community-building and governance. His vision is appealing, but not yet a reality for everyone. It is no secret that fractiousness and incivility pervade the public and private realms. We need look no further than the morning headlines to witness the destructive nature of life in the political arena where the attitude—"We may disagree, but I'm okay, you're okay"—has become—"We disagree. I'm okay. You're a scumbag." A note penned by White House deputy counsel Vince Foster, found in his effects after his suicide on July 20, 1993, offers a bone-chilling perspective on life in the political arena: "Here [in Washington] ruining people is considered sport."[3]

Foster's note suggests that we have a long way to go on the road to a truly civil society. But there are signs of hope. For example, a 1997 article in *Governing* about the politics of ugliness and uncivil behavior by citizens and public officials cites the administration of Cedar Rapids, Iowa, Mayor Lee Clancey as an example of political reform. The heartland city was plagued in the early 1990s by a "circus" atmosphere in which citizens harangued their elected officials and city council members harangued each other. Council members told one another to "shut up"; one member even took to wearing his gun to meetings. Launching "an intensive campaign to restore civility to public proceedings," Mayor Clancey, who was elected in 1995, secured the city council's commitment to a set of 25 operating norms, which govern behavior among colleagues, and 14 core values, which describe what the council stands for. Promising to show support and respect for one another, not to blindside one another, and not to discount each other and the public by their words, gestures, body language, and side-bar conversations, the mayor and council undertook an intensive and open campaign to restore civility to public proceedings.[4]

Civil people, however, do more than speak and act respectfully. As Bill Bradley's vision of a "healthy, robust civic sector" suggests, they engage. Where would Cleveland be if Anthony Pilla, the Roman Catholic bishop of Northeast Ohio, had not had the courage and determination to address the issue of suburban sprawl by mobilizing his constituents to meet with business and governmental leaders to encourage them to focus development back toward the central city and the poorer inner-ring suburbs? Where would Atlanta's 1996 Olympic Games have been without the vision and steadfast leadership of real estate lawyer Billy Payne, who headed the Atlanta Committee for the Olympic Games? Where would Charlotte, North Carolina, be if NationsBank Chairman Hugh McColl had ignored the dilapidated structures and deteriorating public housing on the north side of downtown—rather than assembling whole parcels of it and taking on the role of developer to ensure that new businesses and housing sprang up there even if the market did not seem ready for it? A civic leader is one who cares enough about his or her community to engage in the issues and fight for positive change. So we find today that such persons, in many visible and not so visible ways, are becoming more active in communities across the country—sharing resources and responsibilities, weighing in on new development plans, addressing housing issues, encouraging citizen participation, and nurturing economic development. Civic leadership makes sure all stakeholders are at the table.

In Cleveland, citizens struggling in urban neighborhoods like Hough and Fairfax were hanging banners from the streetlamp posts a few years ago, celebrating efforts of Mayor Michael White's administration to collaborate with grass-roots leadership to promote urban reinvestment, as evidenced by repaired roofs, new windows, new paint, and better-maintained lawns.

On the opposite side of the country, in Portland, Oregon, a citizens' advisory committee played a key role in forming and adopting the city's 1972 downtown plan. Replacement of an ugly expressway along the river with a waterfront park, the building of a well-designed city center, and the development of the light rail transit system would not have happened without extensive citizen participation, including the 500,000 questionnaires mailed to Portland households to request the views of citizens.

In Chattanooga, Tennessee, leaders in the public and private sectors cobbled together $23 million in foundation money, government grants, and low-interest loans from local banks to establish Chattanooga Neighborhood Enterprises, a nonprofit organization that is turning renters into homeowners at an astonishing rate of 500 per year. Two grass-roots organizations, Citizens Organized for Public Service and the Metropolitan Alliance, train citizens to become informed participants in community-building activities in San Antonio, Texas. And in San Diego, the University of California founded an organization in 1985 that nurtures startup technology firms by introducing them to faculty members and research materials as well as to corporate investors. As a result, local biotechnology firms have increased from 44 to 110, communications companies from 36 to 60, and computer firms from 35 to 130.[5]

These examples serve as models for initiatives in other cities across the nation and offer general lessons in the art of civics. As Peirce and Johnson argue in *Boundary Crossers*, "There's no magical leadership structure—just people and relationships . . . no one's excused." They further suggest that "Everyone has to chip in to make the mix work. Universities, professions, faith communities, and the media are top among the candidates to enrich the leadership mix," and that "collaboration is messy, frustrating, and indispensable. Regardless of whether traditional leaders like it, collaboration is here to stay. Once people know they can have a voice, they demand it."[6]

The Demographics of Diversity

Greater diversity in the future, not less, appears to be the message of current U.S. demographics. We stand on the edge of a society more pluralistic than we have known in the past. According to the Hudson Institute, an Indianapolis-based think tank, there will be big jumps in the Asian and Hispanic segments of the working population, from 3 percent and 9 percent, respectively, to 6 percent and 14 percent, and a decline in the white segment, from 76 percent to 68 percent. The African-American proportion will hold steady at about 11 percent. Furthermore, by the year 2020, there will be as many women as men in the workforce, and about one out of every five Americans will be 65 or older.[7]

We cannot consider diversity as a core strength without recognizing a salient fact of American life: We are still a divided nation, white and black, brown, yellow or red, separate and unequal. This is not the place to get into a full-blown discussion of race relations in America, but no book on successful cities of the future could *not* deal with the subject in some manner. The pain and separation that minorities have felt for generations must be understood by leaders at all levels. Leaders must make coming to terms with racial and ethnic tension a high priority if for no other reason than to make their cities attractive places in which to live and invest.

A successful 21st-century city will not sweep the race problem under the rug; it will seek to understand and do something about it. For indeed, "race matters," as Cornel West, professor of African-American studies at Harvard, writes in a book of that name. "A candid examination of *race* matters takes us to the core of the crisis of American democracy. And the degree to which race *matters* in the plight and predicament of fellow citizens is a crucial measure of whether we can keep alive the best of this democratic experiment we call America."[8]

To turn diversity into a core strength instead of a liability, there must be opportunity for upward mobility—not only through the political system, but through the economic system as well. Leaders in the public and private sectors must help women and minorities break through the glass ceilings that for so long have locked them out of top positions. Diversity cannot be ordered up like a sack of groceries. It must be institutionalized from the top down, which involves changes in attitude within an organization's culture. Wider opportunities in the marketplace for women and minorities do not just happen automatically. In 1976, as mayor of Indianapolis, I instructed the city's police department to ensure that minorities and women constituted at least 25 percent of its recruit classes. Over the years, we were able to increase the numbers from 9.8 percent to 18.3 percent for African Americans and from 6.8 percent to 14.9 percent for women. It is my belief that the numbers would not have increased substantially if the system, which favors the good old boys' network, had been left to its own devices.

Some social critics and civil rights activists believe that lawmakers should not only institutionalize antidiscriminatory practices but also force the marketplace to hire a predetermined proportion of employees based on minority status. This view has resulted in affirmative action, which, with its rigid quota system and race-based hiring practices, has become anathema to many who correctly feel that such preferential treatment constitutes reverse discrimination. But does this mean that all efforts to unbar the door that has long locked out minorities should be abandoned? Certainly not. In a society where black families earn less than two-thirds what typical white families earn, some form of legislated program is needed to level the playing field.

Of course, public policies that ensure equal access to employment, education, housing, and health care can help to curtail discriminatory practices. But community builders know that laws address only a part of the problem. Bill Mays of the Indianapolis-based Mays Chemical Company believes that the nation's shift in emphasis from civil and political rights to economic rights calls for a change in leadership, from lawyers and preachers to business owners and workers. I think he's quite right. Minority leadership must offer fewer criticisms and appeals to feelings of victimhood and more programs that provide economic development opportunities, create jobs, and aggregate capital. William H. Harris, former president of Texas Southern University, put the case for black leadership well when he said in a commencement speech: "We in the African-American community must take responsibility for our lives. Only then will we be in position to affect the future of this world. We must take the leadership in rebuilding our cities and communities; we must insist that our youngsters have excellent schools, but also that they attend the schools with excellent deportment and a zeal to learn; we must demand a commitment to law and order but insist that administration of the law be just and equitable; we must insist that young people develop skills that will enable them to work and understand the necessity of having a job, for, as Frederick Douglass told us, 'It is vain if we talk about being men, if we do not do the work of men.'"[9] Perhaps Cornel West puts it most succinctly: "To be a serious black leader is to be a race-transcending prophet who critiques the powers that be (including the black component of the Establishment) and who puts forward a vision of fundamental social change for all who suffer from socially induced misery."[10] Indeed, there's nothing wrong with an ethic of personal responsibility and self-reliance, just as there's nothing wrong with publicly initiated efforts to bolster equality. It takes a combination of both economic and political forces.

"Community Capitalism"

Good leadership knows how to leverage its human capital, whatever its color or creed. *Community Capitalism: Rediscovering the Markets of America's Urban Neighborhoods*, a report produced by the Ninety-First American Assembly in 1997, focuses on how to make capitalism work in distressed urban communities. The Assembly, a regular meeting of representatives from business, academia, the media, labor, faith communities, and government, defines "community capitalism" as "a for-profit, business-driven expansion of investment, job creation, and economic opportunities in distressed communities, with government and the community sectors playing key supportive roles." The group advocates community capitalism not only as a strategy for achieving profitable growth but also for improving societal conditions and overcoming existing economic disparities. The Assembly warns that economic segregation, which has been growing throughout the 1990s, will weaken the ability of metropolitan regions and the nation to compete in the global marketplace. The "key supportive roles" government can play are "rationalizing the regulatory environment, investing in public infrastructure and services that are normally available in nondistressed areas, improving the business environment, and assisting in developing a willing and work-ready labor force."[11]

To promote community capitalism and to rediscover (and recover) the market potential of urban neighborhoods, the Assembly suggests as one possible strategy targeted sourcing, wherein businesses voluntarily purchase from companies located in or employing residents from impoverished urban communities. In Southern Dallas, 300 businesses have voluntarily banded together to report on their hiring and promotion of minorities. Such reporting procedures strengthen peer accountability.[12]

Indeed, there are many examples of businesses that are doing their part to reinvest in distressed central city areas and in the people—the human capital—who live in them. Major national corporations such as UPS and Marriott Hotels have sought to develop a strong neighborhood-based workforce. Other companies have chosen to site themselves in urban neighborhoods, slowly reversing the tide of corporate exodus to the suburbs. In Indianapolis, Indiana Farm Bureau Insurance rehabilitated a 70-year-old tire and rubber factory to house its headquarters in a location near the city's downtown. Local governments, too, are working to enlarge minorities' share of the economic pie through a commitment to increasing the goods and services they purchase from minority- and women-owned businesses. When I was mayor of Indianapolis, we expected 10 percent of our city business would be allocated to minority- and women-owned firms, and that majority firms with which the city was contracting also would have subcontracts totaling that amount.

"A Sturdy Wagon"

During the 1980s, as a result of declining federal and state aid, urban America witnessed the emergence of the entrepreneurial city. Cities looked more to their own resources, discovering that for-profit and not-for-profit organizations in the private sector would make helpful partners in attracting urban reinvestment. By the 1990s, efforts to run cities in a more efficient, business-like manner; off-loading the delivery of some city services to nongovernmental organizations became a popular strategy. It is likely that both of these trends—partnership and privatization—will continue into the 21st century. Government cannot do it all! Public officials have come to appreciate the wisdom of Sir Winston Churchill when he remarked: "Some people regard private enterprise as a predatory tiger to be shot. Others look on it as a cow they can milk. Not enough see it as a healthy horse, pulling a sturdy wagon."[13]

Collaboration between the public and private sectors has led to the revitalization of many cities during the last 20 years, building a platform of opportunity on which to cooperate in the future. Consider an example from Indianapolis. In the mid-1970s, the dream of becoming a permanent home for the U.S. Open Clay Courts Tennis Championships, which had been played in Indianapolis for over 50 years, gained currency among certain governmental, philanthropic, business, and academic leaders as well as among local tennis fans and players. Building a new $7 million tennis stadium soon became the goal. As mayor, I made it clear that the city would participate in the project only if the stadium were located downtown, where it could promote urban reinvestment. Indiana University put up the land, the city allocated $4 million of a redevelopment bond issue to the project, the Lilly Endowment pledged a matching grant of $1.5 million, and 100 companies purchased the rights to box seats at $15,000 a pop. The deal was done because the public, for-profit, and not-for-profit sectors collaborated. If they had not, the project would have failed.

Public/private partnerships have come in for their share of criticism. Critics allege that they amount to nothing but subsidies for businesses that choose to work with government and that public monies would be better spent on education, public safety, and infrastructure. Such arguments cannot answer the But for . . . questions: But for this partnership, what would happen? But for this project, in which new life replaces decay, what would happen to the tax base? But for this collaboration, would the performing arts center or the new sports stadium have been built? But for the private sector's contribution, would this or that government service have to be dismantled or scaled back?

While the matter is controversial, the partnership between government and business to build stadiums for professional sports teams offers an example of collaboration that seems to have contributed mightily to the revitalization of the central city. For the construction of the dome stadium in Indianapolis in the early 1980s, for example, the city council endorsed state-enacted enabling legislation to levy a 1 percent tax on food and beverage served in public places, raising a revenue stream to back a $47.5 million bond. Two philanthropies pledged $30 million toward the project, and the corporate community purchased boxes. St. Louis constructed a modern state-of-the-art facility, the Kiel Center, which is not only home to several St. Louis–based sports teams—such as the professional NHL hockey team, the Blues—but also to the St. Louis region's primary indoor facility for the circus, concerts, ice skating shows, and small conventions. Most events seating fewer than 21,000 people take place at the Kiel Center, located downtown at the insistence of Mayor Vincent Schoemehl, Jr. Financing for the project involved $34.5 million from city bonds and private investments totaling $135 million, which came from privately guaranteed city of St. Louis bonds, bank loans, equity positions taken by the corporations involved in the deal, deposits on suites and club seating, and investment earnings. Indiana University's Mark Rosentraub has called this "an effective public/private partnership . . . as close to a success story as any city can get in the world of sports."[14]

The restoration and rehabilitation of New York City's Grand Central Terminal, scheduled for completion in 1999, is another example of public/ private partnership. This treasured architectural landmark will become a major urban retail center with more than 160,000 square feet of space, housing more than 100 stores, shops, restaurants, and cafés that will serve a daily on-site market of more than 500,000 people. As with the projects in Indianapolis and St. Louis, this revitalization project is made possible by collaboration. New York State is putting up capital funds through the Metropolitan Transportation Authority, while another revenue stream is being created by capitalizing the value of the retail outlets and rents.

The moral of these stories? By working together and bringing their respective resources, tools, and expertise to the table, the public and private sectors can have a positive and substantial impact on efforts to preserve America's urban core.

"The Joy and Responsibility of Making . . . Communities Succeed"

Collaboration in the evolution of our cities means embracing diversity as a core strength. It also means the business community and government working together as partners. Furthermore, it means engaging citizens in the decision-making process. In Spokane, Washington, Mayor John Talbott has invited any and all citizens to comment on the city's strategic planning process for urban revitalization. "Talk about whatever you want," he has told them, with the consequence that he and the city council have received lots of free advice about such controversial matters as getting rid of one-way streets downtown.

To determine and achieve common goals, community builders like Mayor Talbott understand the importance of collaboration, of bringing together citizens and grass-roots organizations with local movers and shakers. Successful city leadership will not permit fundamental decisions to be made by a group of gray-haired white men over a two-martini lunch or on a golf course. The Front Porch Alliance, a program in Indianapolis that allocates public funds to such community-based projects as drug treatment centers, is an example of decentralized decision making. Cited in a *Washington Post* article by columnist E.J. Dionne, Jr., Front Porch serves to "supplement or supplant government programs with voluntary and civic action." Looking askance at programs like this one can result in undesirable consequences, as Dionne warns: "If government doesn't root its activities in citizen efforts, it will be neither fully democratic nor effective."[15]

Understanding that any strategy for urban improvement must include not only local business, labor, and government but also the perspectives of urban and suburban residents, cities will encourage the formation of citizen groups that come together to ask tough questions: What's our vision for this community? How can taxes on new growth be distributed more equitably across a multijurisdictional region? Could there be a better regional response to problems such as crime, water supply, trash collection, and traffic congestion? Do we need more bikeways and greenways in our city? What can be done to address the pernicious effects of racism in our community? How can we do a more effective job of economic development?

Seattle Mayor Paul Schell hopes that the people of his city will accept "the joy and responsibility of making their communities succeed." Consequently, Schell has adopted the strategy of presenting ideas on such topics as transit routes, parks, downtown projects, and neighborhood plans to the public, engaging citizens in dialogue and giving them a chance not just to blow off steam but also to think creatively, to become "coauthors of new approaches." His goal: "tailored solutions, neighborhood by neighborhood."[16]

Seattle's case is no anomaly—citizen involvement works, as millions are proving nationwide. In Richmond, Virginia, more than 500 organizations and citizens have worked together in the neighborhood team process to target issues and resolve problems. Greater Philadelphia First is an economic development consortium of corporate CEOs in the Philadelphia region. Its mission is to bolster the region's economic competitiveness, attract business to the area, and undergird public education; the consortium also has undertaken research that has led to the identification of clusters of business activity on which the city should build—professional services, data-intensive services and products, precision manufacturing, and hospitality and tourism. In Silicon Valley, some 1,000 people participated in forums in the early 1990s on serious problems the Valley faced—in spite of its high-tech wizardry—such as gridlock and schools. This collaborative strategy produced, for example, a unified building code for 29 jurisdictions.[17]

Clark County, Oregon, invites citizens to assist in the preparation of its annual budget. FOCUS St. Louis puts citizens' task forces to work on such salient regional issues as tax equity, school quality, and criminal justice. A team of business, university, and community leaders has turned Austin, Texas, from "a sleepy college town and state capital" into "an internationally renowned technology powerhouse."[18] These efforts and similar ones around the country demonstrate new models for civic engagement, providing mechanisms for people to work together across lines that traditionally have divided them.

And the models are limitless. Consider that community activists can harness the very forces of technology that threaten to isolate us to facilitate civic involvement instead. The Internet is producing an explosion of microdemocracy. People are setting up chat rooms to discuss issues, share ideas, and disseminate information. In *Creating a New Civilization*, the Tofflers describe the world's first "electronic town hall," held in Columbus, Ohio, which they attended. Suburban residents took part via interactive cable television in a political meeting of their local planning commission, registering their views and voting on proposed plans. The Tofflers call this a "primitive indication of tomorrow's potential for direct democracy, using today's far more advanced computers, satellites, telephones, cable, polling techniques," and other tools. Thus, an educated citizenry can "for the first time in history begin making many of its own political decisions."[19]

There is a new breed of civic entrepreneurs emerging—grass-roots leaders who combine two important aspects of the American tradition: entrepreneurship (the spirit of enterprise) and civic virtue (the spirit of community). These citizens motivate (sound the wake-up call), network (secure commitments), teach (present the facts and open minds to new ideas), convene (bring people together and recruit support), drive (press for resolution), mentor (nurture a lasting culture of civic entrepreneurship), and agitate (push for a continuous process of change).[20] The following list provides tips for citizens and local leaders who want to hone their cityship and become involved in shaping their communities.

■ Join or monitor planning boards, code-writing agencies, and zoning commissions;

■ Create a speakers' bureau of talented individuals willing to address local issues at Kiwanis and Rotary club meetings and the like;

■ Learn who's who in local governance, cultivate a good working relationship with them, and offer your expertise;

■ Write letters to the editor, op-ed pieces, and guest columns;

■ Conduct policy seminars to discuss issues in a balanced, factual, nonpartisan fashion;

■ Attend meetings of community-based organizations;

■ Inform peers about issues facing the community;

■ Provide pro bono services to needy community organizations and individuals; and, possibly,

■ Seek public office.

The civics of the 21st century will be more about relationships between people than about structures of governance. "The key is to get people talking and working together across the boundary lines that traditionally divide and diminish a community," advises John W. Gardner, a former cabinet secretary, referring to individuals "from government, corporations, social agencies, ethnic groups, unions, neighborhoods and so on . . . . The citizen leadership we need for the twenty-first century requires a lot of people from every sector working very hard together to make our communities better places to live, work, and raise our children."[21]

Mayor Dennis Archer of Detroit has received high praise for his commitment to the multilevel collaborative approach. First, he has affirmed a partnership between local government and the business community and endeavored to create a business-friendly environment, "rolling out the red carpet" for new investment. According to his office, $7 billion of commercial investment has been made since he was elected in 1994. Second, he has thought and acted regionally, joining the Detroit Regional Chamber to recruit businesses from around the world to the Detroit region. Third, he has committed his city to participating in the global economy. Like other mayors, he has journeyed abroad, from Turin, Italy, to Toyota, Detroit's "Sister City" in Japan, to tell his city's story and garner new trade and investment. He also has held receptions for foreign-owned businesses operating in Detroit; worked with the Japan Business Society of Detroit Foundation; hosted the annual North American International Auto Show, which attracts manufacturers, suppliers, media, and visitors from around the world; and persuaded the Japan-America Conference of Mayors and Chamber of Commerce Presidents to hold their next meeting, in the year 2000, in Detroit. Mayor Archer exemplifies the leadership John Gardner was talking about—getting people to work together across the boundaries that historically have separated them. He shows us that collaboration, not confrontation, is the key to progress.

THE SUCCESSFUL CITY OF THE FUTURE WILL BE
DRIVEN BY COLLABORATIVE STRATEGIES. IT WILL FIND
STRENGTH IN DIVERSITY, PARTNERSHIP, AND CITIZEN
PARTICIPATION IN THE COMMUNITY-BUILDING PROCESS.
THAT IS PART THREE OF MY VISION.

FINDING NEW NEIGHBORS

THE SUCCESSFUL CITY OF THE FUTURE WILL THINK AND ACT GLOBALLY, REGIONALLY, AND LOCALLY

COLLABORATION HAS IMPLICATIONS BEYOND THE ones already discussed. A new era has dawned in intergovernmental relationships. Many observers of contemporary urban affairs have noted that the old paradigm of federal, state, and city is being replaced by a new one: global, regional, and local. Strong leadership will be open to the new possibilities inherent in this transition.

Global

Globalization has been defined as "shorthand for the increasing integration of the world's economies through trade, financial flows, transportation, and communications technologies."[1] The world's boundaries are fast eroding because mobility of knowledge and capital have increased so tremendously. Consider that $67 billion was emptied out of the Bank of Kuwait in *five minutes* when the threat of an Iraqi invasion appeared on the horizon. The key for today is openness— free trade, free markets, instantaneous communication—shrinking distances. Peter Schwartz, a futurist and chairman of the Global Business Network, and Peter Leyden, features editor at *Wired* magazine, are worth quoting:

The key formula for the coming age is this: Open, good. Closed, bad. Apply it to technology . . . business . . . philosophies of life. . . . If the world takes the closed route . . . nations turn inward. The world fragments into isolated blocs. This strengthens traditionalists and leads to rigidity of thought. This stagnates the economy and brings increasing poverty. This leads to conflicts and increasing intolerance, which promotes an even more closed society and a more fragmented world. If . . . the world adopts the open model, then . . . societies turn outward and strive to integrate into the world. This openness to change and exposure to new ideas leads to innovation and progress . . . growing tolerance and appreciation of diversity, which promotes a more open society and a more highly integrated world.[2]

In practical terms, this global openness produces results like these, as compiled by the National League of Cities (NLC):

■ World trade in goods and services is up 13-fold in real terms since 1950;

■ Foreign investments in the United States are up nearly 500 percent since 1980;

■ About 5 million Americans now work for foreign-owned enterprises on U.S. soil;

■ State governments spent almost $100 million in 1990 for international trade, investment, and tourist programs; and

■ One in six manufacturing jobs is linked to exports; however, only one-third of manufacturing firms are currently engaged in exporting.

NLC concludes: "America's cities and towns, in order to prosper in the 21st century, will have to improve their capacity to deal successfully with new international contexts. The most successful will be closely connected to the rest of the world—through trade, transportation, technology, education, arts, and culture."[3]

The successful city of the future will accept the global economy and the opportunities it presents to sell services and do business overseas. A world without borders makes it possible for a city's business leadership to acquire international financing for its ventures, buy supplies, do research and development, and manufacture wherever it can get the job done best and at the lowest cost. Management guru Peter Drucker foresees that "education will become the center of the knowledge society, and the school its key institution," and that this new era will be the most competitive yet "for the simple reason that with knowledge being universally accessible, there will be no excuses for non-performance."[4] Cities will understand that bigger is often inefficient, costly, wasteful, inflexible, and bureaucratic. As John Naisbitt writes in *Global Paradox*, "the smaller and speedier players will prevail on a much expanded field."[5]

"The world marketplace is opening up many opportunities for sales, investments, tourism, and cultural exchanges. The global economy is a reality, and our cities must be ready to seize the opportunities it presents," says Columbus, Ohio, Mayor Greg Lashutka, who has done a magnificent job of opening his city to the realities of the global economy—from having multilingual airport welcome signs and hotel phone book instructions to establishing a city government Office of International Business to help local businesses find international trading partners and to conduct trade electronically. *Fortune* points out that "for many major companies, going global is a matter of survival, and it means radically changing the way they work."[6] Mayor Gary McCaleb of Abilene, Texas, understands that this is also true for cities. "If the global corporation is keeping in touch with technology and market trends all around the world, then responsible city and town officials should do the same." Abilene has established the Mayor's Task Force on Technology, made up of citizens from all areas of the community to identify ways in which technology can serve people. This task force has "created an awareness level in the community for people who didn't even know some of the technologies were here, or that the expertise was here," and helped them "realize ways they can personally and directly benefit from it."[7]

Elsewhere:

■ East Orange, New Jersey, which has a growing population of West African and Caribbean immigrants, has capitalized on and consistently nurtured extensive ties with the nation of Ghana by establishing a student exchange agreement with a university, by setting up a sister-city relationship with Akropong Akuapem, and by establishing reciprocal trade offices and joint ventures with Ghanaian investors.[8]

■ Newport News, Virginia, which has an aggressive program to attract international investment, places ads in European site-selection magazines.

■ Anchorage, Alaska, roughly equidistant from Moscow, Tokyo, and New York, is working to become the international air crossroads of the world, primarily as a hub for air cargo transport.

■ Spokane, Washington, has four sister-city relationships in Japan, Germany, China, and Ireland.

- Colorado Springs has 2,000 acres set aside as a Foreign Trade Zone, which is a legally secured area outside of U.S.Customs territory where foreign and domestic goods can enter the country to be stored, distributed, exhibited, assembled, or combined with other products without duty payment or with the payment delayed, thus significantly improving a company's cash flow.
- Kalamazoo, Michigan, has declared itself TeleCity USA and has become part of the Electronic Global Village project, with the goal of taking advantage of new telecommunications technology to link Kalamazoo to the world and to enhance business, education, and entertainment opportunities for the city. The project enjoys wide support among the business and university sectors as well as among county and state governments.
- Rohnert Park, California, has pledged $120,000 a year to promote the Sonoma County Wine and Visitors Center for the benefit of the wine and tourism industry. One feature: videos available in Japanese and German.
- Japanese is taught in Tuscaloosa, Alabama, grade schools.
- Phoenix, Arizona, has established an international policy committee to guide its global activities.
- Dallas, Texas, has an international Ambassador of Dallas program, in which Dallasites living abroad represent and promote the city on a voluntary basis.
- Charlotte, North Carolina, has created a 35-member Mayor's International Cabinet of public and private leaders to provide advice on international matters.[9]

Globalization has opened new doors of opportunity for cities. Of course, its downside is that it makes one economy more vulnerable to what happens in another. One stumbles, others start to fall also. What happens in Japan affects what happens in Russia, which affects what happens in America, which affects what happens in cities. The best way for a city to protect itself against downturns in a global economy is to have as diversified an economic base as possible. That will give it some resiliency.

The following is a list of steps that cities and their leaders can take to lay the foundation for going global:

- Prepare a globalization plan;
- Promote export of local products;
- Attract foreign investment;

- Internationalize city hall;
- Build on the community's cultural diversity;
- Foster active sister-city relationships;
- Get involved in cultural and student exchanges; and
- Make your city foreign user–friendly.

Regional

We have entered the age of the "citistate," as in ancient Greece. Technology has obliterated the borders of nations, states, counties, cities, and towns. Regions composed of dominant cities and their satellites are now competing against each other. Neal Peirce and Curtis Johnson, cochairs of the Citistates Group, have defined citistate as "a region consisting of a historic central city surrounded by cities and towns that have a shared identification, function as a single zone for trade, commerce, and communication, and are characterized by social, economic, and environmental interdependence." Put more simply, Pres Kabacoff, president of the New Orleans–based Historic Restoration Inc., an organization that plans adaptive use of historic buildings and rebuilding of historic neighborhoods, says such a region "includes all those in a metropolitan area who watch the same six o'clock news, read the same daily newspaper, and go to the same professional sports events." Eighty percent of the American population resides in the nation's 314 regions; 84 percent works in them.[10]

Regionalism is the attempt to think and act in metropolitanwide terms. It is a spirit as much as a structure of governance—formal and informal, public and private, mandated and voluntary, organic, not static. The challenge in the next few years will be to translate regional thinking into regional action, with positive change resulting from intergovernmental relationships and federal and state law. Cooperation on a regional basis will be a key to survival in the 21st century. "Every indicator suggests that the next century will be the century of the region," asserts the National Association of Regional Councils. Regions have become the basic building blocks of the global economy. Regional collaboration will have a significant impact, not only on the quality of life in neighborhoods across the country but also on our ability to compete globally.

In corporate America, it is well known that corporate site selection consultants consider regions, not just cities. Quality of life, access to transportation and utilities, schools, tax rates, clean water and air, and skills in the labor force are all taken into account in location and relocation decisions—and these are regional issues. Businesses have decentralized. New York, Los Angeles, Chicago, Denver, Houston, Pittsburgh, Boston, Atlanta, Washington, Seattle, and San Francisco are only a handful of cities where companies do business regionally. In the Chicago region, most of the Sears Roebuck & Company workforce is located in a distant suburb. In the Indianapolis metropolitan area, a number of Japanese firms have come to locations outside the city proper.

Joan Herron, the Chicago-based member of Atlanta's Lockwood Green Consulting firm, which specializes in economic development and site-location analysis, rightly asserts that cities need to develop a focused regional marketing effort. She cites the case of Decatur/Huntsville, Alabama, where a large Boeing/McDonnell Douglas facility (2 million square feet, 3,000 employees, 500 acres, $500 million) is now under construction. The state and region had put together an incentive package, but it turned out that the facility needed deep-water access with roll-on/roll-off barge capacity in order to transport the huge rockets it manufactures. Since Huntsville, the initial site considered, lacked such access, regional officials looked around for another site and came up with nearby Decatur. Bingo, they had a deal, and regional cooperation was the key.

The regional approach can be as effective in government as it is in business. The Houston region has been wrestling for years with suburban annexation issues, and leaders are now searching for ways in which cooperation between municipal units can occur. Allegheny County, Pennsylvania, has installed a regional asset district to support recreational and cultural institutions and libraries in the whole county (not just the city of Pittsburgh) with revenue from a 1 percent county sales tax. In Sacramento, California, Valley Vision, a regional partnership of business and government leaders, has been formed to develop specific cluster-based initiatives for the Sacramento region. Valley Vision's ambitious goals include holding an economic forum and civic entrepreneur workshops; creating action teams to focus on cluster-specific issues like skills training and economic development, transportation, and land use regulations; forming a Sacramento Valley Public Policy Institute to engage the universities and colleges, both public and private; and persuading the various Valley communities to plan and work together rather than go their own ways. Around Grand Rapids, Michigan, the Grand Valley Metro Council, formed in 1988, unites 29 municipalities and Kent County to do transportation planning and automated mapping for the region.

The simple point is that in regional cooperation there is strength. United we stand, divided we fall.

Resistance to Change

City officials are concerned about entering the 21st century saddled with 19th-century boundary baggage. They would like structures of governance that reflect the times in which we live and the economic and social realities of the regions within which their central cities are located. But for the most part, the interest in governmental consolidations has not caught on. The prevailing attitude is to resist change: "Come weal or come woe, our status is quo." In Wichita, Kansas, a merger of city and county government was rejected by the county commissioners even though the city council voted in favor of the proposal, and even though Bob Knight, the mayor of Wichita, magnanimously offered to step aside as CEO of the merged entity in favor of the county manager. When I visited Wichita, people told me it was "the most overgoverned county in the country." The merger had been proposed by a local task force staffed by Wichita State University and supported by the local newspaper, the *Wichita Eagle,* to overcome the incredible proliferation of governmental agencies in Sedgwick County, Kansas—47 governments involved in road construction and maintenance, 22 in sewer services, 21 in fire protection, 20 in parks and recreation, 18 in law enforcement, 15 in libraries, and 13 in water services! The proposal languished for a while but came to a head again on August 4, 1998. Unfortunately, on that day a close vote had 27,422 citizens of Wichita/Sedgwick County voting in favor of consolidation and 27,596 opposing, so the referendum failed once more.

There are several reasons why resistance to governmental consolidation occurs. First, fear: People quake at the prospect of a rise in taxes and possible loss of autonomy. Often, the hobgoblin of "big government" is raised, fueling the myth that metropolitanwide planning is tantamount to socialism. Suburbanites are also afraid that urban problems will follow hard on the heels of any governmental reorganization.

A second impediment stems from our political legacy. America was not formed from the top down but rather through a compromise between central authority and local autonomy. Local control has always been a sacred right. As Rick Rosan, president of the Urban Land Institute, has observed, "our country is not well organized to do regionalism. We are organized to fail." We have too many jurisdictions, and so much is jealously guarded as a local prerogative (like police and fire departments and schools, to say nothing of property rights) that it becomes difficult to accomplish regionalized services the way it's done in most other countries, where the state handles many of these delivery systems.

The third reason is human nature, pure and simple: More often than not, people resist change. Bureaucrats guard their turf by slowing down or deep-sixing requests for new initiatives that originate "upstairs" in the elected official's office.

Regardless of the reason, the American metropolitan reality is fragmentation of government, with its ensuing inefficiencies and waste.

The Beginnings of Regional Thinking and Acting

Having said this, a little light does shine in the darkness. Regionalism is gaining momentum. The mood is changing. Many are beginning to understand that regional stewardship represents an expression of our collective self-interest. Regional fragmentation and polarization lead to weakness; regional coherence creates strength. Consequently, cooperative bottoms-up ventures are occurring. From the Treasure Valley Institute in Idaho and Wasatch Front in Utah to the Somerset Alliance for the Future and MSM Regional Council in New Jersey, people are joining together to discuss problems that extend beyond municipal borders, such as land use planning, transportation, pollution, and crime. They recognize that none of us is an island; we're all part of the mainland.

Allan Wallis, director of research at the National Civic League in Denver (and a nationally known regionalism guru), has suggested that there have been three waves of regionalism. The first took place in the 19th and early-20th centuries, when major metropolitan areas—such as New York, Boston, Philadelphia, and New Orleans—were consolidated. This wave relied on the political power of central cities over suburbs.

The second wave occurred in the 1960s and 1970s as a response to top-down mandates. The number of federal grant programs supporting state and local planning increased from nine in 1964 to 160 in 1977. Councils of governments, representing more than 90 percent of U.S. counties, increased to more than 660. Special-purpose metropolitan districts were established to provide such regional services as solid waste management, sewage treatment, transportation, planning, and water supply. Consolidations were made, like the merger of county and city government into UNIGOV (Unified Government) in Indianapolis, the Metropolitan Service District in Portland, Oregon, and the Metropolitan Council of the Twin Cities in Minnesota.

In Indianapolis, UNIGOV consolidated city and county governments and centralized public services under a strong mayor system in the late-1960s by an act of the state legislature. The mayor was elected countywide, as were four members of the city-county council; the other 25 council members represented single-member districts. Six departments—public safety, metropolitan development, public works, transportation, parks and recreation, and administration—were responsible for managing city operations and reported directly to the mayor. As a result of the merger, Indianapolis became the 12th-largest city in the country overnight. The merger was far from complete, however. Fire and police services were not consolidated, schools remained independent, tax rates were not unified, and four smaller incorporated areas within Marion County boundaries retained their own city councils, town boards, police and fire departments, and parks.

Wallis suggests that in the 1990s a third wave of regionalism has surfaced, attempting to steer a "middle course" between the centralization of the first wave and the specialization of the second. Here, metropolitan consolidation will in all likelihood not occur. That window, open in the second-wave period, has now closed. This third wave, which has to do with capacity building, moves beyond issues relating to formal governmental structures. It includes informal and private processes to bring people together to discuss common problems, debate policy, form coalitions, mobilize for political action, and deliver services. This will be done in neighborhood meetings, ad hoc voluntary groups, academic centers for urban research, regional partnerships, and chambers and growth associations, as well as through formal public bodies, task forces, and public hearings ("the only place in America where no one listens," as Dan Kemmis, former mayor of Missoula, Montana, is wont to say). The common thread is that participants in this process seek to address the challenges that cut across communities—from crime to drugs, from economic competitiveness to protection of the environment, from transportation planning to job training.

The states and feds can help to move locals in a positive direction by offering incentives and by using block grants to stimulate regional approaches—if not, indeed, by mandating such cooperation. The Intermodal Surface Transportation Efficiency Act (ISTEA) legislation represents the most recent effort on the part of the federal government to require regional planning for transportation funding. ISTEA requires public participation in determining future land use patterns. In Albany, New York, for example, ISTEA prompted the development of a regional transportation plan for the entire capital district (Albany, Rensselaer, Saratoga, and Schenectady counties). Minnesota has area transportation partnerships in each of its seven Department of Transportation service districts for the purpose of developing regional transportation investment programs. The Ada (County) Planning Association provides long-range planning for Boise, Idaho, and its surrounding rural communities.

ISTEA also stimulates public participation in the decision-making process. When St. Louis developed its long-range transportation plan in 1992, three broad-based committees, 200 persons strong, advised the steering committee on land use and environmental concerns, employment and community needs, and regional economic goals. It took two and a half years for the

Dulles Corridor transportation study to be developed for Virginia's Fairfax and Loudoun counties. During that time, five rounds of public meetings at various locations were held, attracting more than 1,200 people. The study was also made available on the Internet, allowing for responses by E-mail, and more than 500 were received.[11]

At the state level, constructive regional cooperation also is being encouraged. Take Virginia, for example. In 1996, the state passed a Regional Competitiveness Act, creating a pot of funds to encourage regional cooperation and partnerships. An area qualifies for a grant when it earns 20 points (ten for tax base sharing, one for joint parks, etc.). Nineteen areas in the commonwealth have become eligible, one of which is Hampton. Its 15 communities, according to former Hampton Mayor James Eason, formed a partnership of private, public, military, and educational leaders to identify strategic issues which, if implemented, can effect improvements in such areas as regional planning and economic development.

None of this is possible, however, without grass-roots support. In a democracy, the people need to be involved! As James Fishkin observes in the *Washington Post,* "Citizens hunger to be consulted in a serious way, but they resent being manipulated or being condescended to."[12] Citizen empowerment—helping people understand that they have a role to play and good input to offer, breaking through bureaucracy, deconcentrating the rigid centralized hierarchy of decision making and making it more inclusive—is required if success is to be achieved.

Regional Civic Organizations

Regional civic organizations (RCOs) are springing up all over the country. These are usually nonprofit 501(c)(3) organizations, created to give citizens a voice in addressing regional problems. For example, the Valley Citizens League in Phoenix oversees implementation of the regional planning process. The venerable Citizens League of Greater Cleveland conducts research on issues relating to a wide range of issues facing that area. Across the country, some 150 Healthy Communities programs have come to life as new-style RCOs to deal with health and quality-of-life issues in local communities. In

the San Antonio region, faith-based organizations are organizing congrega-
tions and citizens to address economic, social, and racial disparities through
the Metro Alliance and the COPS program (Communities Organized for Public Service).[13]

RCOs can be useful in addressing issues that politicians find too hot
to handle. Just try a public discussion of taxing the suburbs in order to equalize the central city burden! In their report on Indianapolis, Neal Peirce and
Curtis Johnson suggest the formation of a new citizens task force, a new RCO
called PEPCI (Panel on Efficiency and Performance for Central Indiana), to
deal with the "hot-potato" issues. It would have to be endowed with authority by the state legislature and the governor, and it would address such matters as fiscal disparities; serious concentrations of poverty and crime; lack of
a serious workforce development plan; division of responsibilities among
cities, townships, and counties; and regionwide economic growth. Ultimately,
the goal would be to study the necessary steps to "create a more cohesive and
efficient Indianapolis cititstate—a region ready to take on the challenges of the
new global economy and serve all of Indiana well."[14] In Houston, under the
sponsorship of the Greater Houston Partnership, a series of forums on regionalism has been held to discuss questions relating to annexation of suburban territory into the city of Houston and the delivery of some services on
a regionwide basis—controversial subjects to say the least.

The connection between RCOs and economic development is too crucial to ignore. Unquestionably, regions fuel our nation's economic growth.
This fact was underscored by a headline in *U.S. Mayor,* published by the U.S.
Conference of Mayors, which reads, "City/County Metro Economies Drive
National Economic Boom."[15] The article points out that the gross product of the
ten largest city/county metropolitan areas in the United States exceeds the combined output of 30 states and that metro areas generate more than 80 percent of
the nation's employment, income, and production of goods and services!

To stimulate economic development, a number of communities in and
around Marion County, Indiana, have signed so-called nonaggression pacts
in which they have agreed not to engage in bidding wars to lure new business from one jurisdiction to another by outdoing each other in incentives

offered. Communities that vie with each other for tax base (i.e., new development) find themselves giving away more and more by way of incentives to attract business. If all in a region would cease and desist, there would be no losers. All would win, because the increase in the tax base ultimately helps everyone. To take another example, the Dulles transportation corridor in Virginia is experiencing explosive growth as its high-tech industries become firmly rooted. By 2020, the number of households and jobs is anticipated to grow by nearly 140 percent and 125 percent, respectively. This could not happen without a long-range transportation plan, because congestion hampers the economic growth of the region. A number of different agencies were involved in the development of this plan, along with a large number of citizens. Why not call the whole process an RCO? Again, the Citizens League of Greater Cleveland endorsed a "sin tax" on alcohol and tobacco in order to help fund Cleveland's highly successful Gateway Project (where Gund Arena and Jacobs Field are located). If the referendum had failed, the project might have evaporated.

What if an attempt were made to counteract the problem of regional fiscal disparities by implementing tax-base sharing? In the Twin Cities, a metropolitan revenue-sharing area has been established, where all municipalities in the district receive a share of the growth of the area's tax base, because each city contributes 40 percent of its commercial/industrial tax-base growth (since 1971) to a regionwide pool. Funds from this pool are redistributed to communities according to a formula based on population and market value of property.

There's no one right way to put together a regional development plan. Each region has unique characteristics; one size does not fit all. If the will exists, people can come together to design a consensual vision for the future of their region and then develop the governmental and financial tools to implement it. Regionalism does not mean metropolitan consolidation. The arguments that it means more and bigger government, increased costs to the taxpayer, and loss of local control are bogus and demagogic. Regionalism simply acknowledges that finding lasting solutions to borderless problems like crime, drugs, poverty, the flight of wealth and brainpower to the suburbs, irresponsible land use, pollution, crumbling infrastructure, and downtown decline will take all hands working together across an entire region.

Balancing Regional and Local Priorities

The trick for regionalists is to satisfy simultaneously two public goods that seemingly conflict—namely, local control of quality of life versus the value of cooperating together across local lines. It's the same problem that the founding fathers and mothers faced: consolidation, fragmentation, or both? Retaining local identity without being overwhelmed by big government is one worthy goal; gaining efficiency and becoming more competitive by transcending parochialism is another. The key question: Will we act like scorpions in a bottle or bees in a beehive?

Some believe that an urban federal system is the happy medium.[16] If a region's municipalities recognize that the real city is the entire metropolitan area, they need to find ways to work together without sacrificing local control, property rights, and a voice in government decisions. They must steer a middle course between consolidation and balkanization. Houston has been identifying "the specific goods and services that should be assigned to smaller jurisdictions, and those where responsibility by larger jurisdictions is more efficient, effective, equitable, and accountable."[17] This produces a strong regional government that has the resources to address and resolve major regional issues and a system of local jurisdictions or "villages" that have control over the services of most vital concern to their residents.[18]

Probably those goods and services that have large capital costs associated with them—sewers, bridges, port authorities, resource recovery systems (trash collection and disposal), water systems, airports, public hospitals, museums, stadiums, thoroughfares, and highways—will have to be treated regionally. Those that are more labor intensive and do not benefit so much from economies of scale—police and fire departments, parks, schools, social services—will have to continue to be provided locally.

Short of full-blown metropolitan organization, are there ways of governing our regions better? Of course! There are cooperative intergovernmental agreements, single-purpose special authorities and districts, councils of governments, coordinated planning agencies, multiservice authorities, and annexations, before a community arrives at regional consolidation. The narrower the range of function, the easier a particular form of regional governance is to accomplish; the broader, the harder.

Examples of these intermediate steps abound. Joint planning and funding of new infrastructure, joint purchasing agreements, and sharing of recreational facilities are common.

■ In Indianapolis, there are mutual-aid agreements between different jurisdictions' fire departments.

■ In 1978, Portland, Oregon, established, through state legislation and voter three-county and 24-municipality Metropolitan Service District, which provides services ranging from solid waste disposal to operation of the zoo and convention center and performs a wide variety of planning activities in such areas as land use, economic development, and transportation.[19]

■ A special service district was created in Denver to help finance Coors Field, a new ballpark.[20]

■ Seven counties in Maryland developed a memorandum of understanding to alert neighbors (prior to public announcement) to forthcoming changes in plans and regulations.[21]

■ In Kentucky, Louisville and Jefferson County entered into a compact in 1986 that provides for sharing revenue from several sources and clearly delineates which entity will provide a dozen different activities.[22]

■ The Mandan-Bismarck-Burleigh-Morton Joint Service Network in North Dakota has been established to "concentrate on government functions and services that might be better provided together rather than separately."[23]

■ In the Dayton, Ohio, region, arts and cultural agencies in the city and county have forged an alliance called the Montgomery County Arts and Cultural District to develop cooperative strategies and spend $1 million annually in sales tax revenue.[24]

■ The city of Houston has granted a few local jurisdictions—such as the Greenspoint and Galleria Management Districts and the Lamar Terrace Tax Increment Reinvestment Zone—the authority to provide additional services above and beyond what the city provides.

All these instances fall short of complete consolidation as in Nashville, Tennessee/Davidson County, where seven municipalities and one county were merged into a single metropolitan government in 1963. The need for these intermediate alternatives is clear. In his report to Denver's Metro Forum in December, 1991, Chairperson John Buechner said: "The Denver metropolitan area does not have in place a governance structure that can effectively solve critical regional issues, including water, transportation, air and water quality, solid waste, health care, and open space."[25] Cities will need to consider ways of cooperating among neighbors not only to offset decay and improve services but also to stay vital and competitive in the coming century.

Implementing Regional Strategies: Asking the Tough Questions

The questions we need to ask ourselves about regionalism range from hard to easy. Tax-base sharing is probably the most volatile issue that regionalism faces. The next most controversial is regional land use planning. The easier issues probably have to do with service delivery—namely, regional cooperation to permit economies of scale and savings to the taxpayer. A community that seeks to weigh the benefits of regional cooperation, or, already convinced of its merit, wants to move forward and develop a plan, might begin by asking the following questions:

■ If a regional economic development agency were set up, with, say, the city, the chamber, and the state as partners (as is the case in Indianapolis), could a more effective job be done in retaining and attracting business to a community?

■ In the area of labor force preparation, private industry councils around the country are bringing private-sector leaders together with government officials and service providers on a regional level to combine forces in developing job training programs. Does our community need a private industry council?

■ Could a municipal bond bank be set up to pool issues, reduce issuing costs, and earn higher rates of return? For the same reasons, would pension funds be better invested if they were pooled?

■ What if regional fares were coordinated, as in the Puget Sound Region, so that users could transfer between bus, ferry, rail, and vanpools using only one card, rather than different cards for each system?

■ Could crime be more effectively fought if a region consolidated some of its crime-fighting equipment, like a crime lab or automated fingerprinting machine, or local police and fire radio frequencies, or emergency telephone answering services?

■ What is our community doing to implement database sharing among schools, libraries, or public transportation agencies, now that electronic networking has become so widespread?

■ Could a regionwide trash disposal authority be established that would dispose of solid waste in an environmentally safe manner, rather than having a multitude of municipalities dumping in separate landfills?

■ Could a regional service authority (there are some 3,000 nationwide, employing 400,000 people, with budgets totaling $15 billion) handle a region's solid waste disposal, stadium construction, water supply and treatment, port services, transportation, air pollution control, and parks management?

■ If a development produces leapfrogging sprawl, should an effort be undertaken to stop it? How about establishing growth boundaries, as in Portland, Oregon? Or declining to provide public infrastructure for bad sprawl?

■ What if an attempt were made to counteract the problem of regional fiscal disparities by implementing tax-base sharing, as in Pittsburgh and Allegheny County, Pennsylvania?

We cannot abandon hope. The fight for regionalism is worth the candle. At stake is the health of entire metropolitan areas and the future of the American city.

Neighborhood

The saying that all politics are local also applies to land use and development. States and feds may pass laws, but their impact is local. Everything occurs at the local level, or, more accurately, in the neighborhood. "Neighborhoods are the building blocks of a successful region," write Peirce and Johnson. "If they are weak and socially unstable, a dark shadow is thrown across the entire citistate future."[26] Cityship understands this.

Urban neighborhoods are characterized in different ways. In Indianapolis, for example, they are sometimes denoted by boundaries, like a river, street, or park (Meridian/Kessler); sometimes by a geographical location, north, east, south, or west (the Old Northside); sometimes by a style of architecture (the Warehouse District); sometimes by their demographics (German Park); and sometimes even by a famous name (Butler/Tarkington). Regardless of definition, a neighborhood is a clearly identifiable place where people live or work within a larger community.

It is perhaps a sign of the times that *Emerging Trends in Real Estate 1998* points to traditional neighborhood development as the newest "market to watch." The report states forthrightly: "Sample the attitudes of suburbanites today and you'll find a growing number who think their lifestyle is becoming more difficult and less appealing" and "for the first time, they're considering alternatives." Traffic congestion seems to be driving this trend to a large extent. People are simply tired of spending so much time "trapped in their cars" and seem increasingly to be favoring stores and town centers "within easy walking distance."[27] This suggests that the paradigm may be shifting away from suburban sprawl to neighborhood-based communities. No wave of migration back from the suburbs has yet appeared, but glimmerings of it can be discerned in reports like *Emerging Trends*.

Usually, a neighborhood's residents are proud to live there and are willing to work hard to safeguard their investment and quality of life. Throughout America, neighborhood-based organizations work tirelessly to preserve the vitality of their special place, trying always to hold the line against decay. These efforts often are undertaken by nonprofit organizations in collaboration with the public and private sectors. All kinds of programs are sponsored to achieve this end: beautification of parks, installation of street amenities, orchestration of cultural activities, conversions of old buildings, acquisition of vacant land, demolition of boarded-up housing, and many more.

Preserving Neighborhood Vitality

A city cannot revitalize itself all at once. Counteracting deterioration has to be done one step at a time, neighborhood by neighborhood, targeting areas of manageable size. "How do you eat an elephant?" "One bite at a time," goes the answer. Where low-income neighborhoods are concerned, they not only can be revitalized, but actually have assets that can create growth. It is important for local governments to help to provide incentives for the private sector by making it easier to invest in homes, jobs, and businesses in these neighborhoods, and by providing the basic infrastructure of services: sewers, parks, streets, sidewalks, libraries, schools, public safety, and out-patient health clinics. A free-market approach to neighborhood revitalization—creating capital—makes more sense than one characterized by income redistribution.

The Trust for Public Land in San Francisco published the *Guide to Recycling Vacant Property in Your Neighborhood* in 1979 for neighborhoods struggling against blight. It suggested seven steps for the acquisition and recycling of vacant land in a community:

1. Get organized for action.
2. Identify lots to be acquired.
3. Acquire the land.
4. Organize and incorporate your neighborhood Land Trust.
5. Plan and design the site together.
6. Prepare and develop the site.
7. Maintain and preserve the community-owned property.[28]

One example of recycling vacant land: Indianapolis and other cities put some of their smaller parks, or "tot lots," up for bid in the hope that neighborhood- or faith-based organizations will adopt them. To cite a more complicated example, in the South End of Niagara Falls, New York, the main shopping street is Pine Avenue. A vacant lot became available along the avenue, and the Neighborhood Housing Services program approached the Pine Avenue Business Association (PABA) with a plan to lease the lot for 20 years in exchange for paying the $400 annual real estate taxes. The PABA contributed about $8,000 for lumber, hardware, and landscaping. The city provided grading and subsoil work and contributed about $7,000 of community development block grant money in order to prepare the site. Thanks to the neighborhood's vision and determination, a very successful neighborhood park came into being.[29]

In the mid-1980s, St. Anne's Hospital closed its doors on Chicago's West Side. A community-based development corporation, Bethel New Life, knew that this inner-city neighborhood's spiral of decline would continue if the building were left to rot. It put together a multimillion-dollar package of public and private funds, acquired the site, renovated about 80 percent of it (335,000 square feet), and renamed it the Beth-Anne Life Center. Now, in place of the blight, there exists a small business center and training facility, 125 residential units for seniors, an office building, a branch bank, a drugstore, a performing arts center, and a health care facility. None of this would have happened without Bethel New Life's combination of neighborhood commitment and business acumen. Thanks to this organization's determination to recycle worn-out land, out of failure, a success was born.[30]

The following list provides tips for cities seeking to spur neighborhood revitalization:

- Maintain infrastructure (sidewalks, curbs, sewers, streets, bridges, parks);
- Promote self-sufficiency and homeownership;
- Plan for mixed land uses;
- Make any new development harmonious with what's already there;
- Cluster economic development in nodes along underused commercial corridors;
- Provide a full range of community services;
- Find new uses for abandoned land and old buildings;
- Create open spaces, amenities, parks, and streetscape improvements;
- Undertake beautification programs in storefronts and homes;
- Mix moderately priced with high-priced homes in villagelike communities;
- Ensure the safety of all residents;
- Make good schools a priority;
- Make available public transportation that guarantees residents access to jobs in other parts of the city;
- Use the full range of funding available from the public and private (both for-profit and philanthropic) sectors, in addition to tax incentives and loan programs; and
- Deconcentrate poverty, and do not segregate by race or class.

The Role of Intermediaries

In a discussion of neighborhoods, the role of intermediaries should not be overlooked. There are investment banking organizations (usually not-for-profit) such as the Enterprise Foundation, founded by the late visionary developer from Baltimore, James Rouse; the Local Initiatives Support Corporation (LISC); the Neighborhood Reinvestment Corporation; and the Community Development Corporations (CDCs) that pump new financing into poor neighborhoods to promote homeownership and other revitalization strategies. Technical assistance, counseling, and networking are also offered by these intermediaries, which are very creative in their use of low-income housing tax credits, grants, and loans. They usually ask local corporations and businesses for a substantial commitment that they then match with funds raised nationally.

The AFL-CIO's Housing Investment Trust and Building Investment Trust, both intermediaries, invest in more than 300 pension funds, mostly union. A 1994 estimate was that the $1 billion or so the two intermediaries had invested since their founding had created 31,000 residential units and nearly 3, 000,000 square feet of commercial property.[31] New York City's Community Preservation Corporation, a consortium of banks created in 1974, arranges below-market loans for developers of affordable housing. The well-known South Shore Bank in Chicago was America's first community development bank. The bank has lent more than $400 million to more than 11,000 inner-city businesses and individuals since 1975—and the bank has been turning a profit each year to boot! The New Community Corporation, a community-based development organization in Newark, New Jersey, was founded after that city's 1967 riots "to restore the spirit and fabric of life." This intermediary has built or rehabbed 2,500 housing units for 6,000 residents annually and has placed about 1,000 low-income people in full-time employment every year. NCC operates a high-volume supermarket and job training programs for area residents. The result? These revitalization efforts "have brought private investment in housing and business back into central Newark."[32]

CDCs are not without their critics, who point out that some do at best a mediocre job and spend subsidies without results. They also are disliked by some who feel they block out the private sector by developing projects through their not-for-profit mechanisms. However, there are now several thousand CDCs producing hundreds of thousands of new and rehabilitated units of housing. That translates into millions of square feet of commercial /industrial space and more than 100,000 new jobs.

In the "Peirce Report on St. Louis," which appeared in the *Post-Dispatch* in mid-March 1997, Neal Peirce and his colleagues scold the city for failing to work with LISC and the Enterprise Foundation.[33] While St. Louis forsook intermediary involvement, Kansas City was receiving $172 million in development dollars available to CDCs through an intermediary's efforts, Chicago $444 million, Cleveland $152 million, Detroit $49 million, and Indianapolis $82 million. This is a boat worth catching, because intermediaries and CDCs are at the heart of neighborhood revitalization efforts throughout the country.

An interesting and important initiative that puts a for-profit twist on neighborhood revitalization through job creation is known as "Social Purpose Enterprises." A nonprofit organization sets up a for-profit subsidiary to provide jobs for the inner city unemployed, and not just coincidentally, additional revenue for the nonprofit. Pittsburgh and San Francisco have well-established SPEs up and running. In Buffalo, New York, the Clarkson Center, a job training nonprofit, created its Energy Control Management subsidiary in 1996, which now provides four services—catering, home insulating, retail, and janitorial—that employ some 50 people, generate sales of about $1 million, and will turn a modest profit this year of approximately $50,000. Funding comes from the organization's own pocket as well as from private-sector support. Again, wealth creation, not income redistribution, is the key.

The Role of the Urban University

One cannot address the subject of neighborhood revitalization without discussing the role of urban universities, which are sometimes criticized for not being constructive participants in the affairs of their own communities. They offer a substantial employment base, to be sure, and turn out productive citizens (the motto of the University of Indianapolis is "Education for Service"), but they argue and disagree in their academic circles about the role that urban universities should play. "How little we do," laments former President

Jimmy Carter, "to share the greatness of a university with a poverty-stricken family half a mile away."[34]

In reality, many universities offer cities and regions tremendous resources and leadership. They can—and do—practice cityship. In my hometown, Indiana University/Purdue University at Indianapolis (IUPUI) not only provided the leadership for such worthwhile community organizations as the Greater Indianapolis Progress Committee but also manifested its interest in being part of the city's efforts to revitalize neighborhoods and support leadership-infrastructure empowerment and development within the community. This 25,000-student institution formed the Community Outreach Partnership Council to focus its resources on three low-income neighborhoods adjacent to the campus and to strengthen community ties. Saint Louis University made a conscious decision not to move out of the city, reaffirmed its role as an active partner in the rebuilding of the area around the campus, and in 1996 provided more than 218,000 hours of service in programs ranging from tutoring school children to aiding senior citizens. The University of Missouri in St. Louis has a Center for Excellence in Urban Education and a Regional Institute for Science Education, where faculty members work with 5,000 area teachers and students. Similarly, Washington University in St. Louis involves faculty members in a science education partnership with local public schools. At Texas A&M, faculty and students have helped residents of nine "colonias" (pockets of dire poverty peopled by Mexican Americans) to create community centers that now sponsor youth activities, job training programs, and nutrition education, drawing on cooperative efforts by 160 public and private agencies. In Chicago, Loyola, DePaul, Chicago State, and the University of Illinois have formed a policy action research group to work with some 20 community-based, citywide social service organizations, engaging students working with community mentors on more than 130 projects around the city, in every policy area from welfare reform to housing rehabilitation to determining what it takes to maintain racially and economically integrated neighborhoods. Dr. Carl V. Patton, president of Georgia Tech, talks about "combining academic excellence with urban relevance . . . . Because of our resources and location, we have an obligation to address the issues and problems of all urban areas." Dr. Patton proposes three action items for urban universities: shape public policy, provide resources, and serve the community.[35]

True, urban universities exist to educate, not to save the cities, but the successful city of the future will harness their power and expertise to do the three things that Dr. Patton suggests. Name a great city and it will undoubtedly serve as the home of a great urban university. The challenge facing cities is to connect with urban universities so that one more positive step can be made in bridging the gulf that separates "a technologically adept, globally connected, well-paid elite" from "classes of people with little education and bleak career hopes in the new world economy."[36]

LEADERSHIP REACHES FROM NEIGHBORHOOD TO REGIONAL TO GLOBAL. IT WORKS WITHIN THE FRAMEWORK OF THE NEW PARADIGM. THAT IS PART FOUR OF MY VISION.

MINDING THE STORE

THE SUCCESSFUL CITY OF THE FUTURE
WILL BE MANAGED EFFICIENTLY AND EFFECTIVELY

LET'S BEGIN BY DISTINGUISHING BETWEEN efficiency and effectiveness. Efficiency has to do with doing things better, smarter, less expensively. The 1990s have been years in which government at all levels has sought to perform more efficiently. At the national level, there is the Vice President's performance review task force trying to reduce paperwork, cut red tape, simplify personnel systems, and control costs. At the state level, Florida's review commissions look every 20 years at its constitution and every ten at taxation and budget practices. Indeed, according to David Osborne, coauthor of the best-selling *Reinventing Government*, by the mid-1990s, 39 states reported quality initiatives, 29 indicated at least some efforts to measure performance, 28 said they were seeking customer feedback, more than 30 were simplifying their personnel systems, ten were experimenting with eliminating budget line-items, and ten were testing competitive public-versus-private bidding for service delivery."[1]

The same trend can be observed at county and municipal levels of government. City after city is attempting to streamline its operation, hold the lid on tax increases, and outsource some of the workload to the private sector through competitive bidding. Cities are measuring performance, reviewing outcomes, benchmarking, forming quality circles, and moving to activity-based costing. In Indianapolis, we established a PEPPER (Public Entrepreneurship, Productivity, Privatization, Efficiency, and Restructuring) Commission, and my successor followed it with SELTIC (Services, Efficiency, and Lower Taxes for Indianapolis Commission). These commissions, composed chiefly of corporate managers, accountants, and CEOs, illustrate how government is reaching out to business for assistance in becoming more efficient.

Of course, government cannot be run like a business, but it can be run in more business-like fashion. Its first job is to mind the store well. Just as in business, in government the process of restructuring, reforming, redesigning, rightsizing, and "reinventing" (to use the current buzz word), can cut costs, eliminate wasteful spending, avoid duplication of functions, and train employees to become more quality conscious and customer oriented. The traditional, highly centralized command-and-obey, turf-protecting system that has characterized governance during much of this century can and should be changed so that local government can serve its customers better than it often does. I recollect visiting one large city for a meeting of professionals in the land development business, and when I made a comment about how unresponsive the local mayor's office was to my efforts to get in touch with the mayor, several others around the table chimed in with similar stories about phone calls not being returned, letters going unanswered, and so forth. Not very efficient! That's probably why Peter Drucker wrote, in *Innovation and Entrepreneurship* (a book I gave to all 29 members of the Indianapolis City County Council in 1985), "To build entrepreneurial management into the existing public-service institution may thus be the foremost political task of this generation."[2]

The general idea is that government should do more steering, less rowing. That is, government sets policy, but does not need to mount huge programs to implement policy if it can farm out the responsibility to a private-sector vendor. The days of throwing more and more dollars at a program have passed; the days of trying in every way possible to give taxpayers more value for their dollar have arrived. This fundamental paradigm shift is moving cities in new and exciting directions. It involves such strategies as:

- Outsourcing service delivery to private-sector vendors (privatizing);
- Practicing a style of management called "learning government," in which "trust and lead" replaces "command and obey," with the goal of empowering employees and building self-sufficiency and creativity;
- Bidding out to private-sector firms government delivery services like chuckhole repair and street sweeping, instead of keeping all those responsibilities in public-sector hands;

- Focusing on the needs of the customer, not the bureaucracy;
- Measuring outcomes rather than inputs; and
- Load shedding—asking what we can do without because it is not essential to our mission.

These ideas have been fully explored in such excellent books as *Breaking Through Bureaucracy* by Michael Barzelay, *Reinventing Government* by David Osborne and Ted Gaebler, *Banishing Bureaucracy* by David Osborne and Peter Plastrik, and *The Twenty-First Century City* by my successor, Stephen Goldsmith. In his book, Goldsmith outlines a "few simple principles" that have guided his decision making:

- People know better than government what is in their best interest.
- Monopolies are inefficient, and government monopolies are particularly inefficient.
- Wealth needs to be created, not redistributed.
- Government should do a few things well.
- Cities must not raise taxes or price themselves out of competition with excessive regulation.[3]

Effectiveness has to do with whether the measures undertaken in the name of efficiency actually help government fulfill its obligations to create a safe, well-ordered, healthy community in which to live, work, and raise a family. It would be efficient (i.e., save taxpayers money) to pick up trash monthly instead of weekly, but it might not be very effective, particularly in the summertime. The art is to deal effectively as well as efficiently with the myriad problems that local government faces in this time when people are demanding that the size and scope of government be shrunk.

Security

A developer wrote me a letter in 1997, saying he would not go into the central city to work on any project until that city had solved its problems of crime and education. Every poll of public opinion and public officials indicates deep anxiety about crime. Concerns about personal safety play a role in people's decisions about where they are going to live—and the central city usually loses out. Public safety issues appear near the top of every budget and list of priorities in America's cities. Just last year, the National League of Cities declared building safer cities one of the major items on its agenda, citing growing concerns about juvenile crime, drugs, and violence.[4]

The major portion of our nation's fight against crime is carried out by government, chiefly by local governments, leaders, police, and citizens. Mayor Rudy Giuliani of New York has taught us that crime can be reduced by going after the minor infractions as well as the major ones: removing litter, abandoned cars, and graffiti; arresting people who jump over subway turnstiles; moving squeegee wielders off the streets; clearing public spaces of disorderly conduct; and so on. This has been called the "broken-window" theory of crime prevention: By fixing the broken window, you overcome the appearance of deterioration and chaos that provides the seedbed for crime. Professional apartment managers, for example, can assist in crime prevention by mending the "broken windows" on their properties.

The nationwide trend toward community policing is taking police out of their patrol cars and putting them in greater touch with the community through foot, bicycle, and horse patrols; decentralized roll call sites; and neighborhood substations. Modeled after Japan's kobans, police ministations—neighborhood booths where officers are close to and mingle with residents—are also gaining currency. Another form of community policing can be found in safe havens, spaces like stores, libraries, and schools where kids can find security after school, in the evenings, or on weekends.[5]

Criminologist Timothy D. Crowe, an advocate of crime prevention through environmental design (CPTED), advances the theory that "proper design and effective use of the built environment can reduce the fear and incidence of crime and thereby improve the overall quality of life."[6] Development of defensible space, environments that inhibit crime by creating the physical expression of a social fabric that defends itself, falls squarely on the shoulders of architects and developers, who have an opportunity to address this matter every time they undertake a project.[7] Design sensitive to crime prevention is an important ingredient of municipal growth policies and plans for the creation of new communities. Successful cities will find ways to build an awareness of crime-sensitive and crime-preventive techniques into the planning process for new buildings and developments. City planners, private-sector developers, elected leaders in local government, and law enforcement officials will come together to discuss ways that crime can be prevented through design. This issue will be approached proactively, at the front end of the planning process, rather than reactively at the back end, after projects are completed.

In Ft. Lauderdale, Florida, police actively participate in the design review process. In Sarasota, crime prevention through environmental design is considered part of the city's comprehensive planning process. The city has regulatory requirements that help to prevent or combat crime, such as height maximums on solid barriers. In the Vancouver area, planning staff provide general comments on safety issues when they consult with developers and architects, who also are encouraged to meet with local crime prevention personnel to review development proposals. Multifamily, commercial, and industrial rezonings are referred to the Royal Canadian Mounted Police Crime Prevention Unit, where an officer trained in crime prevention through environmental design reviews applications of site and building plans, with comments referred directly to applicants. In New York's Port Authority Terminal, once a hotbed of drugs and prostitution, the Project for Public Spaces brought vendors in from the street and relocated them in attractive, portable kiosks at entryways where people gather. Their physical presence and the legitimate business traffic they bring to the area function as an effective crime deterrent.[8]

There is virtually no limit to the applications that can be specified with an eye toward crime reduction: increasing lighting and viewing angles; eliminating hiding places; providing alternative walkways that allow people to keep away from areas or other people they do not care to approach (example: surrounding elevator waiting areas with glass walls and doors instead of solid ones); limiting access to high-rise office buildings by not permitting the parking garage elevator to go up to the office areas, or routing all ground floor exits through a common point; putting police substations in malls as well as in neighborhoods; running horse patrols in parking lots; and using technological advances to provide unobtrusive surveillance.[9] This list is by no means exhaustive.

The challenge is to create environments that enable people to manage their own safety and security effectively. It is a truism among architects and developers that design influences behavior, so growing concerns about personal security present them with an opportunity to respond creatively and artfully.

It is probably a fact of 21st-century life that urban control zones and gated communities—suburban fortresses, if you please—will increase. "There is a near-vacuum of compelling, well-tested design approaches" to these zones, according to architect Thomas Vonier, who specializes in security-related design. He argues that we are living in an era when the questionable safety of unrestricted public access should not be ignored. The successful city of the future will adopt "measures to control access, detect threats and deter incidents."[10] It will be characterized by such things as well-policed streets, parks and pedestrian walks, vehicle-free zones, gates, admission controls, fences, hidden surveillance systems, and low-key but omnipresent policing, as in the Disney theme parks or Colonial Williamsburg.

Gated communities usually result in upscale, socially homogeneous, and highly regulated neighborhoods that have little interaction with the rest of the town—part of a growing phenomenon that former Labor Secretary Robert Reich calls the "secession of the successful."[11] (An exception, according to Mayor Willie Brown, is Hayes Valley in San Francisco.) These developments move healthy street life indoors, as it were, and off public sidewalks and spaces. People who live in these communities sometimes go so far as to claim they should not pay property taxes to the city for city services. These more secure enclaves may sadly become America's 21st-century response—just like the walled cities of the Middle Ages—to the prevalence of crime and random violence in our society.

Education

The main challenge of the early 21st century will be the development of human capital. We will be competing in what is shaping up to be World War III (economic, not military!) with Asia, Europe, the Soviet Union, and even emerging countries. The responsibility of cultivating human talent is shared by families, education, and government, so cityship will prompt support of public school systems, primarily in rural and central city areas, since the suburbs and private schools usually possess sufficient affluence to obtain the teachers and equipment they need. The urban inner city is a repository of overlooked talent, and the kids there are not doing so badly, either. According to recent statistics, completion rates (through the 12th grade) are high, and dropout rates are quite low (11.1 percent in 1996, in contrast to 14.6 percent 25 years earlier).[12]

Having said this, the popular perception is that the public schools, particularly urban and rural ones, are failing. We have all read the articles about U.S. kids scoring lower on tests than their counterparts in Singapore, Tokyo, and Berlin. We see on television nearly every day a story about school violence. We visit schools that are in a sad state of repair. Indeed, there does seem to be a crisis.

I wish mayors had more authority to deal with school problems. A mayor is held responsible for just about everything that goes on in the city, especially tax rates, which are heavily affected by school levies. So why deprive mayors of a greater say in how things are run? In the mid-1990s, the Illinois legislature gave the mayor of Chicago greater power over running the Chicago school system, and Mayor Richard M. Daley's accomplishments have been considerable. School reconstruction has proceeded apace, bureaucracy has been trimmed, discipline has been strengthened, the fiscal house has been set in order, huge debt has been erased, student learning has increased, and test scores have inched up. According to the Chicago Public Schools' Office of Accountability, math concepts and problem-solving results for the ninth through eleventh grades (combined) show a nearly 50 percent improvement, from 21.6 percent above the national norms in 1990 to 31.2 percent in 1998, while reading comprehension for grades three through eight (combined) jumped from 23.5 percent to 34.3 percent above national norms in the same time period.

Reform proposals are legion, and all seem to aim at breaking down the government monopoly of the school system to "allow competition to force improvement and innovation."[13] Two of the most prominent reform efforts are charter schools and vouchers, both designed to give parents and students more choice. Charter schools are publicly funded but independently run. Parents opt for charter schools because the schools have the freedom to innovate; they are not rule-bound and procedure-heavy, and they minimize administrative and regulatory burdens. According to the Hudson Institute, "operational freedom in exchange for improved results is the central concept of charter schools." Perhaps that is why teachers' unions and Washington bureaucrats in the Department of Education feel so threatened by them. Hudson conducted a survey of 2,978 charter-school parents in the 700 or so charter schools around the country and found that after switching to a charter school, parents of special-ed youngsters reported a 21 percent increase in children performing at "excellent" and "above average" levels, and a 33 percent decrease in children in the "below average" and "poor" categories.[14]

If charter schools create what one teacher calls a "program of success," vouchers allow public school children to attend a successful school of their choice. Vouchers use either public or private dollars to enable parents to choose the school they want their child to attend, with the dollars following the student.

How America's children are learning, what they are learning, and how much they are learning compared with other countries are important subjects, but they lie a trifle far afield for this book. Nevertheless, there are substantial reasons why leaders of 21st-century cities should be concerned about education in our country. Three reasons in particular come to mind: competitive advantage, taxes, and neighborhood revitalization.

Education and Competitive Advantage

The nub of being competitive lies in job readiness and in matching workplace needs with workforce skills. Given the dependency on welfare that is encouraged by various public policies and given the already-dismal state of urban education, this is not an easy task. It is hard to encourage people on welfare to make the transition to workfare when they can command a higher benefits package on welfare than at a beginning average wage.[15]

There are two keys to making this transition effective. The first is the development of a market-based competitive system of job training, like the America Works program. America Works is a for-profit job training agency that gets fully paid only after a client works in a real job for six months. As

Mayor Goldsmith describes it in the Indianapolis program, America Works places candidates in entry-level jobs, receives their salary for up to four months, pays the employee between $4.75 and $6.00 an hour, supplemented by a transportation subsidy and by daycare provided by the welfare department. For putting a welfare recipient back into the workforce, America Works receives a $5,000 payment. Since the start of the program, 15,000 people have been placed in permanent jobs, 500 of them in Indianapolis.[16]

Unlike a government monopoly that focuses on bureaucracy and spending, this program concentrates on the customer and avoids the one-size-fits-all mentality. The same principle could apply to other social service delivery systems: Government monopoly is neither as efficient nor as effective as market competition.

The second key to workforce readiness and the reduction of poverty is, of course, education. The end result of education ought to be the production of a marketable mind and heart—that is, men and women trained to compete in today's world but also committed to getting up in the morning and rolling up their sleeves for a full day's work. Anyone interested in competing in the 21st-century global economy should be concerned about the failure of our public schools to prepare students adequately for this competition. In Indianapolis in 1997, 20,000 jobs were open in the metropolitan area, yet thousands of residents were still unemployed. "We have a mismatch between jobs and qualifications that only education can correct," writes Mayor Goldsmith.[17]

The problem is not that the public school children are harder to teach, as defenders of public schools sometimes assert. It has to do with the way schools are managed, how much money flows through to the classroom, how cumbersome the bureaucracy is, how many pupils are assigned to each teacher, and what is being done—or not being done—to remove trouble-making students from the classroom to some sort of alternative schooling. Regardless of the cause, we have a serious problem in our country. In a recent national survey of employers conducted by Junior Achievement and Amway to glean their impressions of high school seniors entering the workforce, the employers responded that:

- 27 percent of seniors do not have good basic math skills;
- 21 percent do not work well with people of varying backgrounds;
- 35 percent are not very punctual or dependable;
- 21 percent have only minimal computer skills;
- 30 percent do not understand the importance of getting work done on time;
- 24 percent can barely read a training manual, if at all;
- 27 percent barely get by when communicating verbally;
- 50 percent cannot communicate very well through writing; and
- 60 percent do not know much about how business works.[18]

Not very ready for global competition, would you say? *All* businesspersons in our country have tremendous self-interest in improving our nation's public schools. Officials will have to stop thinking of schools as buildings, of pupils as interchangeable pawns assigned to those buildings by distant bureaucracies, and of school years as having a set time frame. Dismantling the schools' monopoly power; decentralizing them; reducing bureaucracy; giving principals and teachers of local schools more authority; giving parents and students more choices about which schools they attend; returning to core curriculum subjects such as English, math, science, geography, and history; emphasizing achievement in curricular matters rather than socialization skills; privatizing such functions as transportation and school cafeterias; and capping escalating school tax rates are all ways of addressing the problem head-on. These attempts to bring constructive change to America's schools hinge on two basic premises: that there is nothing wrong with competition, and that national performance standards are appropriate.

Someone who believes this strongly is J. Patrick Rooney, chairman of the Golden Rule Insurance Company in Indianapolis. Consequently, he has initiated a program that has been replicated in 31 other cities around the nation, with ten to 15 more in the pipeline. He calls it the Educational Choice Scholarship Fund, started in his hometown in 1991 with his own and the company's money. It is the "first privately funded voucher program for the benefit of low-income, center-city children," Rooney says. To qualify, the child has to be eligible for the federally subsidized lunch program. Rooney matches parents' dollars up to $800 on a one-to-one basis; the cap on this amount makes it possible for a greater number of low-income parents to participate. In Indianapolis, more than 1,300 children are enrolled in the program, with another 1,925 on the waiting list.

Rooney also has started what he calls safe haven schools, for which Golden Rule is providing computers equipped with educational software. These schools are designed to meet the needs of single mothers for a "safe haven" to care for and educate their children. Run by center-city churches, using Sunday school space for classes, they are open from 6:30 a.m. to 6:00 p.m. 12 months a year. Now they run from K-3, but they are expecting to add a grade per year. It seems to me that these two examples from Rooney's work illustrate the kind of innovative breakthroughs that can occur when business and community leaders think outside the box and are willing to work with the public sector to get projects going. They manifest cityship at work.

Property Taxes

In most communities, school taxes take the largest portion of the tax dollar, considerably exceeding the monies spent on local government operations and debt service. In Indianapolis, 44 percent of the property tax dollar goes to the school system (of which only about 30 percent actually makes it into the class-room), 21 percent funds the police and fire departments, and 9 percent supports "everything else city government does."[19] Schools are almost universally funded by property taxes, so it stands to reason that people who pay property taxes have a justifiable concern about what they're getting for their money. Successful cities of the future will figure out how to decrease the dependence of education funding on the property tax.

Nonetheless, school-age population is on the rise, and this will be reflected in the increasing need for construction and renovation of educational facilities, for which the public will have to pay. The U.S. General Accounting Office has estimated that repairs and replacements worth $112 billion are needed to restore our nation's schools to good condition. According to the American Institute of Architects, surveys of school administrators indicate that new school buildings average about 100 to 150 square feet per student; with construction costs averaging about $100 per square foot, the per-student cost of new school facilities is $11,000 to $13,000.[20] The National Center for Education Statistics predicts that enrollment increases will require 6,000 new schools nationwide by the year 2005.[21]

Schools and Neighborhood Revitalization

Deteriorating schools and the physical blight afflicting them do a disservice not only to the children who are being educated inside them but also to the neighborhood where they are located. In Chicago, Mayor Daley has said that two institutions define a neighborhood: the parish church and the school. It is inconceivable that preservation of a reasonably healthy quality of life, much less the revitalization of an older neighborhood, can be achieved without holding the line on school decay.

The TriBeCa (40 blocks in the triangle below Canal Street) neighborhood in lower Manhattan has become a trendy, high-priced area in the past 15 years. Property values have soared as much of the area has been rezoned from manufacturing to residential and commercial. The area has become a mecca for fine dining, and families are knocking at the doors trying to find housing. There are several reasons for this rejuvenation, of course, but one of the most important is the high quality of schooling available in the area. Public School #234, with kindergarten through fifth grade, is housed in a modern, air-conditioned building. It has a well-stocked library and an individualized assessment system instead of traditional formal grading. TriBeCa's nonprofit Washington Market School, an early childhood center influenced by the Montessori method, is operating at full capacity, and a new, combined elementary and middle public school was scheduled to open in the fall of 1998.[22] What has happened in this area is proof that good schools can be anchors for good neighborhoods, magnets that attract and hold families and prevent destabilization of the neighborhood.

TriBeCa, however, is one of the few success stories. Many school districts in America face a double problem of aging structures and rising enrollments. Consider the following examples:[23] In Los Angeles, a majority of the school buildings are more than 40 years old. Since their schools are neither wired to accommodate computers or air conditioning nor equipped with modern security and telecommunications systems, the city's 670,000 students (with an increase of 15,000 to 18,000 annually) are hardly getting a fair shake of the educational tree. Two hundred and forty-five schools need roof replacement, 50 need boiler replacement, 400 require playground repaving, and 600 need repainting. New York is experiencing enrollment growth of 20,000 to 23,000 students per year, yet more than half of its more than 1,000 school buildings are at least 50 years old. In Broward County/ Ft. Lauderdale, Florida, the fifth-largest school district in the nation, 34,000 students are without permanent desks; 10,000 new students are added to that system each year. In Philadelphia, the school district estimates it will need two-thirds of a billion dollars to bring its 257 building sites (60 of which are more than 70 years old) up to standard. When the First Lady took a tour of some public schools in the nation's capital, she was shocked at their condition. (She could have found the same neglect and disrepair in any number of urban school districts throughout the land.) Washington, D.C., schools opened three weeks late in 1997 because of the acute disrepair of some school buildings. Four months later, an audit revealed that "the shoddy contracting system" for these roof repairs "put honest school employees in 'compromised positions' and led to $7.2 million in additional costs as the work was rushed to completion."[24]

Public and Private Sector Involvement

The federal government can provide seed money to kick-start the process of renovating urban schools. In 1997, the Clinton Administration announced a school construction initiative, and sent the Partnership to Rebuild America's Schools Act of 1997 to Congress. In its 1998 version, the legislation proposes federal tax credits to pay interest on nearly $22 million in bonds to build and renovate schools. The bonds would be of two types: school modernization bonds, half of which would be allocated to the needs of the 100 school districts with the greatest numbers of children living in poverty, and qualified zone academy bonds, to be used for a variety of expenses (including building renovation) related to certain public school/business partnerships. Congress is scheduled to act on the proposal during 1998.

At the state level, Governor Parris Glendening of Maryland says that for every $10 his state allocates for new school construction, it is now spending about $8 on renovating or expanding older schools in older communities. "That means science labs and computer centers in those older schools will be just as good as those in our newer schools, and young families will want to send their children to these schools." He adds: "We cannot expect parents to keep their children in schools in our cities or older suburbs if the schools in the newest, far-away suburbs are the only ones with better or more up-to-date facilities."[25]

In the private sector, companies, chambers, and business groups can adopt a school, donate technology to it, or set up a mentoring program for students. This is done in Indianapolis through the Chamber's Partners in Education program. In Boston, local companies have a compact with the city's public schools: If your students graduate from high school with good grades, good attendance, and good deportment, we will give them first crack at a job (assuming they do not go on to college).

What else can the private sector do to help the public schools? Could corporate support be garnered for school construction, similar to what Andrew Carnegie did for libraries a century ago? Could members of the private-sector lobby "jawbone," write articles, and speak out to build support in the business political communities for school construction and reform? In Indianapolis, corporate leadership assembled itself into a group called CLASS (Community Leaders Allied for Superior Schools) to stimulate thinking and action about reform in the public schools. The initiative has metamorphosed into the Educational Choice Charitable Trust, building on Pat Rooney's original idea. The trust raises money in the private sector to fund a voucher program and currently has some 5,000 children on a waiting list. Could private support be enlisted for a greening of the schools, a program that would clean the yards and playgrounds around schools, keep the grass and shrubs and flowers and trees from dying (very much the way private organizations adopt parts of roads and highways), thereby instilling more pride in the neighborhood? Could schools be kept open nights and weekends for other activities, some of which would be underwritten by private companies (like Saturday morning English/Japanese classes, for example)? The challenge is to take responsibility and get involved, for the problems with our schools can not be solved by the public sector alone.

Housing

Most Americans still want to pursue the American dream: a detached single-family house in the suburbs with lots of grass, good schools, relative security, lower taxes, and community amenities a short car ride away. Add to that an office space of some kind, since about a third of the workforce will be doing some telecommuting, and the dream is complete.[26] *America's Real Estate*, published by the Urban Land Institute in 1997, indicates that "[a] growing percentage of the nation's residential stock is in single-family units, which constituted about 68 percent of residential units in 1995. Another 26 percent of residential units were in multiunit buildings, and about 6 percent were mobile homes."[27]

So home building and homeownership will continue to thrive, with rehabbing occupying a larger share of the market. Remodeling expenditures for home improvements (as opposed to maintenance) have grown significantly over the past several years and are expected to keep growing, driven in part by an aging housing stock and strong turnover in the housing market. With the graying of America's population, more attention will be paid to built environments that meet the wants and needs of the elderly who are not institutionalized. As a result of consumer demand and market forces, a "dynamic convergence between the seniors' housing and healthcare sectors" is occurring, according to publicity recently generated by the eighth annual National Investment Conference for the senior living and long-term care industries. Such housing will take different forms: resort or leisure living, continuing-career living, and health-care living.

Concurrently, urban America is witnessing a revival of downtown housing. We'll have more to say about that in a following section, but I think a trend has started in the 1990s that will continue into the 21st century. An article in the *Denver Business Journal* in 1994 claimed that "after years of losing residents to the 'burbs,'" Denver was enjoying "a miniboom" in downtown housing. That has not abated in the years since. "Center-city housing is hot," said the article.[28] The revival is being driven by single-person households, Generation X-ers, and married couples with no children living at home.

In Atlanta, the Techwood and Clark Howell homes (1,081 seriously deteriorated public housing units) are being replaced by a 900-unit mixed-income development with 40 percent of units for sale at market rates, 20 percent for tenants whose income is up to 60 percent of the area median income, and 40 percent for the poorest families. The project is being financed through a $42 million urban revitalization demonstration grant from HUD, private tax credit partners, and private FHA-insured mortgage debt. The housing authority of the city of Atlanta is developing the project together with the Integral Partnership (a joint venture of the Integral Group and McCormack Baron and Associates). To attract market-rate renters, units in the plan are finished with features comparable to other market-rate properties in the area. Early leasing of the five-phase project, which will include a K-5 magnet school and a retail development, indicates a successful mix of incomes.

Between 1970 and 1990, the foreign-born population of the United States grew by about 10 million; by 2010 it is expected to increase by an additional 11.3 million.[29] Some cities, typically gateway cities, have seen their populations begin to grow again as a result of this immigration. New York City, for example, which lost 10 percent of its population during the 1970s, saw its population grow by 4 percent in the 1980s, due in large part to its 28 percent foreign-born population. Similarly, Seattle regained 5 percent of its population in the 1980s as the percentage of foreign-born residents increased, and Los Angeles, with a 38 percent foreign-born population, saw a 17 percent population increase in the 1980s.[30]

Some two-income families with little spare time are trading their commutes for the convenience of the city, particularly in places like Washington, D.C., and New York City. Twenty-somethings seek city locations, attracted by the pace and excitement of the city. At the other end of the spectrum, the aging of the U.S. population is creating new demand in the city for retirement and assisted-living facilities. Many older persons, lacking personal transportation, prefer the convenience of living near public transit, shopping, and medical care. While there is not a wholesale rush to return to the city, the exodus has at least slowed.

Housing patterns will continue to reflect a disparity between haves and have-nots, with the middle class getting squeezed out to a large extent. The average incomes of the households in the top quintile grew 44 percent from 1968 to 1994, while during the same period the average income of the bottom quintile grew just 8 percent.[31] Our family used to live in the Gold Coast in Chicago. Not far away, Cabrini Green, the public housing project notorious for its crime and stockpiling of families on welfare, rose ominously on the western horizon. All around us were wealthier people who could afford the neighborhood's high-priced services and taxes. We could not, and had to move away. Similarly, my son, who lives in New York, tells me that the polarization in that city is becoming so exaggerated that he thinks the middle class is truly vanishing. The end result of this trend in the 21st century may well be the resigned coexistence of the poor and the wealthy in the center cities of America.

An alternative to this might be co-housing, the housing of unrelated families under the same roof. In co-housing, for example, three single parents with their children would share common areas and responsibilities for housekeeping, child care, and cooking, with each group retaining its own private space. Not a traditional family, to be sure; but then, family structure today is less traditional than it used to be, and some people will be willing to sacrifice a little privacy for the sake of convenience and cost. The Nyland Co-housing Community was started in 1990 by a small group of Boulder-area residents who formed the Co-housing Development Company. The company hired the Boulder-based Wonderland Hill Development Company to serve as project manager. Completed in 1993, Nyland was the first co-housing community in Colorado and is the largest in the country to date. The 42-unit project includes a 2,500-square-foot community house with a kitchen, living/dining space, and a daycare area. Most of the residents are middle-aged adults, but there also are about 40 children and a dozen residents over the age of 60.

Race will continue to play a part in where people decide to live. Sociologists and researchers tell us that "whites' willingness to move into a neighborhood is inversely related to the density of blacks living there," while "blacks prefer integrated neighborhoods, but ones with a substantial representation of blacks."[32] Such segregation may be ameliorated by a decline in discrimination among most Americans, who are increasingly willing to buck the trend and live together with people of different ethnic backgrounds, and by the fact that economic status—and not race—is becoming a determining factor in choice of housing.

Debate will continue about the extent to which America should be a country where no one is ill-housed. HUD Secretary Andrew Cuomo has predicted that if Section 8 housing subsidies for poor working families, the elderly, and disabled Americans were to expire, 6 million people could be homeless by 2002.[33] HUD has a number of programs—housing vouchers, HOME grants, homeownership zones, Home Bank loan guarantees—to aid low- and moderate-income people on their trek toward homeownership. But these programs often strike fear into the hearts of people who live far away from the central city. I recall a political campaign in which I was involved in 1979, when my rather moderate support for Section 8 and scattered-site housing was used against me and against a candidate I supported for City Council by race baiters who pandered to the prejudices of white suburbanites.

The consensus on the national goal of affordable housing for all seems to have collapsed, as is made clear in a very compelling monograph by Charles Field of the National Association of Home Builders.[34] Field defines affordable housing as "physically adequate housing that is made available to those who, without some special intervention by government or special arrangement by the providers of housing, could not afford the rent or mortgage payments for such housing." To resolve conflicts about where affordable housing should be located, Field suggests choosing a middle ground between providing no guidelines and dictating policy: undertaking "principled negotiation," a form of joint problem solving developed at the Harvard Program on Negotiation, which is run by Roger Fisher, William Ury, and their colleagues. As a model of the positive possibilities of this process, Field cites a "fair-share agreement for affordable housing" developed for the 29 jurisdictions in the Hartford, Connecticut, region with the help of third-party mediators. Ultimately, each community could tailor its strategies and actions to fit its particular political and economic situation. The solutions, Field says, were to be chosen, not imposed. One cannot help but wonder whether successful cities of the future will undertake this kind of process to restore consensus and move forward toward the legitimate goal of affordable housing for all.

Homelessness, the most extreme of all housing problems, often can be more effectively addressed by the private sector than by government. In Indianapolis, we thought the solution to our city's 1,500 homeless on any given night lay in expanding the private sector's capacity to provide them with appropriate services and shelter. As the director of our Homeless Network remarked: "City governments have not been very successful at running shelters." Many factors contribute to homelessness: mental illness, domestic violence, addictions, chronic poverty, job instability, unaffordable housing, rising living costs, single-parent households, and restricted entitlements. While the private sector cannot solve all these problems, a private-sector task force such as Indianapolis had could spur the creation of day programs for homeless adults, uniform data collection by shelters, referral points for families seeking shelter, citywide screening of the homeless population for infectious diseases, collaboration among mobile health and mental health teams, and coordination with the city for long-range planning and disbursement of federal funds. As a result of this initiative, 147 new beds were created for the homeless, for a total of 670, which seemed adequate for a city the size of Indianapolis, and a day center was constructed to provide social services to the homeless with assistance from the Salvation Army.[35]

The successful city of the future will also help tenants in public housing move from dependency to self-determination. This usually means letting them take charge and have a say in the operation of their units. Placing public housing communities under grass-roots leadership and management has not been a universal success, by any means. But Kimi Gray, a well-known neighborhood leader in Washington, D.C.'s Kenilworth-Parkside neighborhood, has said: "Under resident management, we reduced crime, welfare dependency, recidivism, teen-age pregnancy, vandalism. We increased rent collections and set up businesses that employed residents. As the residents became confident in their ability to improve living conditions, they began seeking a more permanent stake in the future of the community. Homeownership . . . was our dream also."[36] The Kenilworth-Parkside public housing development offers "a dynamic example of what can be accomplished when layers of bureaucracy are removed and real community control is achieved."[37]

One of the country's most successful examples of tenant participation can be found in Boston's Harbor Point project, jointly operated by a private developer (Corcoran, Mullins, Jennison, Inc.) and the community's residents. This redevelopment of the largest federal public housing project in New England reserves one-third of its 1,283 units for low-income rental housing and involves tenants on a day-to-day basis in what has become "a true legal partnership." The Harbor Point Community Task Force, a nonprofit residents' association, owns 50 percent of the project and makes 50 percent of the decisions. Harbor Point contains a mixture of market-rate and affordable housing. The amenities include parks, neighborhood play areas, free parking, shuttle service to nearby public transit and upscale recreational facilities. Social programs such as tutoring, job referrals, health care, services for the elderly, and a youth center are provided. Private officers make the area secure. All this adds up to the dramatic transformation of a dismal failed public housing project into an economically and racially integrated apartment community in an attractive, affordable neighborhood.

In Indianapolis, HUD's urban homesteading conserved central-city housing stock by selling homes for $1 to people who promised to put their sweat equity into them for three years. The houses had appeared on a HUD payment-default list, and we attempted to make them viable anchors in the neighborhood once again rather than boarded-up shells. About twice a year we held lottery drawings for these houses, which were in great demand. At each session, about 30 were usually purchased by potential homesteaders. During the course of my 16 years in office, several hundred such properties were privatized and revitalized.

Indianapolis also has a Neighborhood Housing Partnership to make home mortgages available at below-market rates. Combining philanthropic dollars with public funds and for-profit private sector contributions, the organization works with CDCs (community development corporations) throughout the city to provide housing financing and counseling. In one neighborhood, the partnership helped to transform 83 vacant, boarded-up properties into rental houses.

Another mechanism that the city welcomed was the HODA—home ownership development account. Its purpose was to provide tenants with an opportunity to become homeowners by allowing them to build up credits for paying their rent on time, keeping their property in good shape, completing a homeownership training series, and the like. Each $50 credit was matched by the Eastside Community Investments organization at a ratio of 9:1. Some of those funds came from philanthropic sources, but much of the money originated in development-fee income that the organization set aside for the tenant's account. The HODA was accessible only for specifically approved uses, such as major capital improvements to the home, purchase of major appliances, additional down payment or principal payment on the loan, or discount points for permanent financing. Thus, the tenants who were given the opportunity to hold assets would have an opportunity to clear up their credit problems and ultimately make a down payment on a home. The program has recently been deactivated, but the principle behind it is sound.

The development of infill housing on parcels of vacant land that have been bypassed by earlier development or are left with structures that have deteriorated or been torn down is essential to urban revitalization. "In many cities across the United States, once-vibrant neighborhoods are pocked by parcels of vacant land . . . or are left with structures that have deteriorated or been torn down. Local governments are often eager to see such land redeveloped. And, especially where the demand for housing is strong, developers are looking to use infill sites to create housing that appeals to a diverse housing market, including downtown workers."[38] Infill housing—be it attached, detached, high-density, or low-density—can revitalize urban areas because it reintroduces "affordable, contextually designed housing" into inner-city neighborhoods where there is underused or abandoned physical infrastructure. Such a program is "pivotal to the long-term health not only of our inner-city neighborhoods and future generations of residents but also of our cities."[39]

For example, in the Watts section of Los Angeles, 114 two-story, detached, market-rate houses on 13.7 acres, known as Santa Ana Pines, have given moderate-income households "the first opportunity to purchase a new single-family house in this community since 1985." This infill housing project, yet to be completed, was financed by a group of private investors, with the city providing "soft seconds" through Community Redevelopment Agency and community development block grant funds.[40] In Redmond (home of Microsoft), Washington, the municipality has set a goal of developing some 3,000 housing units during the next 20 years, of which Trammell Crow Residential's mixed-use development, LionsGate, with a density of 35 units per acre, is the first tangible result. This pedestrian-friendly project has apartment units above ground-floor space reserved for home businesses, and has "rented up really fast," according to the city's planning and community development director, Roberta Lewandowski.[41]

In Chicago, Homan Square represents a dramatic neighborhood turnaround with the help of considerable infill housing. This 55-acre redevelopment of the former Sears Roebuck and Co. headquarters in Chicago's North Lawndale neighborhood has been spearheaded by the Shaw Company. Partnering with these private-sector entities, the city made substantial infrastructure investments to support the project. It now consists of nearly 600 units of affordable housing in a secure residential setting; 1 million square feet of commercial space to attract new businesses and employment opportunities to the neighborhood; and a host of social services, such as family support programs, recreational activities, job training, health care, and daycare. Only the huge old Sears Catalog building was torn down; the other buildings were all renovated. Homan Square would not have happened were it not for the strong belief of the development manager (Shaw) and the financial partner (Sears) in the enormous rebound potential of an inner-city neighborhood. But the good news is that revitalization did occur on Chicago's West Side, and relatively low-density infill housing and commerce have replaced deserted, obsolete buildings. Instead of having a site become a cancer on an entire neighborhood, Chicago now has a catalyst for improvement there.[42]

Mount Pleasant Homes in Cleveland, Ohio, provides an example of the successful development of housing on scattered infill sites. The partnership of the Zaremba Group, Inc. with the nonprofit, community-based Mount Pleasant Now Development Corporation and Lutheran Housing Corporation developed 50 new single-family homes on vacant lots that the city acquired through tax foreclosure. The project is the first newly constructed home development to be offered on a lease/purchase basis in Cleveland. Financing for the $4.2 million project includes $3.; million in equity from the National Equity Fund (the nation's largest syndicator of federal low-income housing tax credits); a $400,000 loan from the city's 1992 Housing Trust Fund; a $2 million bridge loan from the state of Ohio; and a 15-year tax abatement from the city of Cleveland. A construction loan of $3.5 million and a $1.25 million permanent loan were provided by Huntington Bank. Because of the city's subsidy, rents are within reach of families that earn as little as 30 percent of the area median.

In Indianapolis, we had two unique programs to bring infill housing to blighted parts of the city. One was a competition we sponsored with the Ball State School of Architecture, giving awards to young architects for the best designs for infill housing. Several houses were built along California Street in the downtown area and sold at market rate. The other was a program sponsored by the Chamber of Commerce and the Indianapolis public schools, giving high school students training for the building trades and an opportunity to build with their own hands central-city market-rate infill housing. These houses came on line at the rate of one every year.

Lots of other examples of infill development could be cited, but the point is clear: Infill housing projects can contribute to the revitalization of inner-city neighborhoods by enhancing their residential character. There is a market niche here if the location is attractive and the design harmonizes with the neighborhood.

Cities can help the private sector to promote homeownership by the way they plan and zone. Charles E. Fraser, a community builder in Hilton Head, South Carolina, is critical of the tremendous regulatory impediments to the realization of good communities. He despairs of "the neighborhood wrecking business created by spot zoning, which is often handed down from town council allies previously bought off with campaign contributions of slick lawyers," by urban bulldozing, and by corporate planning departments "plopping gasoline stations on corners of fine old residential neighborhoods within a month after fifty-year-old, residential-use-only land use covenants have expired." Fraser challenges leadership in the successful city of the future to write and support adoption of new codes for government agencies to follow in permitting growth on metropolitan edges and in the center; and in succinct and beautiful terms, he describes the threshold upon which we stand: "Despite all the obstacles, the coming decade and century can be the Spring Time of the Human Spirit for those serving the nation and their own economic welfare by designing good places for Americans to live, work, play, workshop, and live as families or mature adults in peace and safety".[43]

Vernon Swaback, an architect in Scottsdale, Arizona, has recently written an insightful book, *Designing the Future*, in which he condemns "an unholy alliance" and "unintended conspiracy" between builder/developers who thrive on repetition and avoid exploring anything beyond the obvious "success" of the past, citizen-activists who prefer opposition to any change over selective support for something that might break or set precedents, and city agencies "that take comfort in the fail-safe quantification with which they process formulated criteria for everything from street widths and turning radii, to drainage provisions and lighting standards." These three influences "insure mediocrity" by discouraging or precluding any special use. "The collective result," concludes Swaback, "is that one subdivision looks like another, shopping centers have become standardized and more and more streets all look the same."[44]

The successful city of the future will allow more special uses and not require so much uniformity. Bureaucracies tend to be rigid in their decision making. "Well, you have a good idea but we can't let you do it, because the next person will also want a variance, even if his idea is no good." Successful cities will break through such a mentality to encourage flexibility and train midlevel employees in planning and zoning departments to make distinctions between plans that are high-quality and ones that are not. Such cities will be characterized by the ability to think anew and act anew, figuring out ways something can be done, not excuses for why it cannot. Only with this shift in attitude to allow variance for excellence will a city avoid the race to the bottom, where everything is leveled down instead of up.

A significant initiative in this vein is the conversion of office buildings, warehouses, stores, and hotels to housing, a trend that is gaining momentum throughout the country. Loft-style condominiums and apartments, whether in converted warehouses or new buildings, have become the housing of choice for young professionals and older empty-nesters. Lofts can be found in warehouse districts and new developments in Fort Worth, Tucson, and Chicago.[45] All over America, new uses are being sought for abandoned land and obsolete buildings, which enjoy the advantages of being centrally located and costing less to rehabilitate than new construction would cost.

The city of Denver regarded preservation of the 350,000-square-foot Denver Dry Goods Building as "critical to the health of downtown." The building occupies the entire frontage of California Street in downtown Denver and is strategically located where the 16th Street pedestrian/transitway mall joins the city's new light rail system. The old department store had been closed, and the building sat vacant, deteriorating day by day. The city bought the property, developers from the private sector responded to the requests for proposals, and now the building houses 51 units of affordable and market-rate rental housing and 66 for-sale luxury condominium units, together with retail and office space.[46] In Portland, Oregon, an abandoned dairy was converted into 85 apartment units, more than half of which are reserved for residents who earn less than 60 percent of the area's median income. It also includes 26,000 square feet of retail space on the ground floor. Renamed Belmont Dairy, the project used an unusual array of financing sources, including tax credits, city and state funds targeted to transit-oriented development, venture capital, and bank financing. The ten-story Builders' Exchange Building in downtown San Antonio, Texas, constructed in 1925, was converted to apartments after sitting vacant for more than ten years. The 41 units include nine 350-square-foot efficiency apartments and a mix of one-bedroom, two-bedroom, and studio units. Approval of the project was made possible by the city's support and flexibility in applying modern building codes to a historic property.

The successful city of the future will convert some of its underused or unused space to a new market-driven use: housing. It will recognize the importance of incentives designed to encourage the private sector to participate in the process. "Unlike the cash subsidies of the past, many newer incentives involve removing institutional obstacles that serve as disincentives to private redevelopment and offering tax abatements and other reductions in cost to enhance financial feasibility." Such incentives will include: "changes in zoning ordinances and building codes that remove some of the risks and costs of renovating older buildings, zoning variances, flexible application of building code requirements, property tax abatements, assistance in financing, environmental cleanup, and improvement of the infrastructure."[47]

At an Urban Land Institute Mayors' Forum in Dallas in February 1997, cohosted by Mayor Ron Kirk, we heard a lot about reuses of obsolete buildings and abandoned land. Mary Fishman, director of design for Chicago's department of planning and development, portrayed in vivid and exciting terms the city's program to encourage conversion of storefronts to housing in neighborhood commercial districts. Architecturally significant buildings are preserved in the process, and streetscapes are made more user-friendly. The city reviews zoning and other regulations in targeted neighborhoods to facilitate use of the program. Key issues in implementing the storefront program include providing privacy, light, and ventilation; the size and shape of the interior space; the need for zoning changes and special use permits to convert to residential use; parking; and the need for street improvements.

Mayor John Antaramian of Kenosha, Wisconsin, who also attended that meeting, described how, with the help of a ULI advisory services panel, his city had adopted the Harborpark Master Plan to transform an abandoned manufacturing plant. All that remained was a 42-acre concrete pad with weeds growing through the cracks and some 26.5 acres of grassy land fronting beautiful Lake Michigan. The plan's objective is to create "a high-quality public environment" that will become a new civic and cultural focal point for Kenosha, a family-oriented destination on the lakefront. The plan proposes that a new water-oriented residential neighborhood with full amenities be built, including 220 to 300 new residential units that will provide a variety of owner-occupied housing types, such as townhomes and garden apartments.[48] The kickoff celebration for the implementation of the plan was held on June 13, 1998.

Transportation

When thinking about cities, transportation, and the future, it is useful to approach the subject from three vantage points. First, mass transit use will grow slowly. As measured in passenger miles traveled, it has grown an average of 1.3 percent per year since 1985—but that does not mean alternatives to the solo automobile should not be explored and developed.[49] Second, more development will be oriented toward transportation in the future. Residential and commercial development around transit stations is being encouraged in a number of cities, among them Washington, D.C.; Portland, Oregon; Atlanta; and Chattanooga, Tennessee. In general, though, this phenomenon is limited to older, urban areas. Third, airports are where the action will be. International cargo ton miles increased 122 percent between 1980 and 1990, from about 2.5 million to 5.5 million; passenger miles grew 117 percent, from 54.5 million to 117.7 million.[50]

Mass Transit

In an ideal world, Americans in the next century would make a much stronger commitment to mass transit. This, however, presupposes people living in high-density environments or not having a car, and those conditions are not prevalent. The St. Louis region experienced a 3 percent increase in population between 1980 and 1990 (the city's population declined), but the transit share of commuters went down, from 6 percent to 3 percent, while the use of private vehicles increased from 89 percent to 92 percent. In Phoenix, the percentages remained constant at 2 percent transit, 89 percent private vehicles. In Atlanta, the transit share of commuters decreased by 2 percent. Statistics for other American cities tell the same story.

There are plenty of reasons for this. The American love affair with the automobile is still robust; as our country has matured, the love affair has turned into an enduring marriage to which we have adapted our living patterns. Funding for mass transit is not politically popular in most places, because taxpayers fund the subsidies for mass transit. And then there's suburbanization. Americans have been moving to suburbia in droves since World War II (suburban population grew from 23 percent in 1950 to 47 percent in 1990, while central city and rural population declined by 4 percent and 20 percent, respectively), resulting in low-density sprawl that makes mass transit less feasible—and, therefore, less desirable. Further, job growth is occurring on the edge of cities, and people are working in more diverse locations than they used to. Such decentralization lowers demand for higher-capacity modes of transit.

Except for this: Because the central city is no longer the main growth area in a community, the issue of suburbanites commuting to suburban jobs has become a serious challenge to town planners. ULI Senior Director Robert Dunphy, also chairman of the Transportation and Land Development Committee of the Transportation Research Board, a part of the National Academy of Sciences, believes that in most growing areas, getting people to downtown jobs is no longer the major preoccupation. The problem is much more diverse, involving commutes made entirely within the suburbs for work and shopping, as well as the usual off-hours traffic.[51]

While cities have many options for getting people downtown, the choice for most suburban destinations is only one—the car. Consider the case of Washington, D.C. By the year 2020, the number of vehicles is expected to increase by 7.4 million, to a total of 20 million, a 60 percent increase over 1990 levels. Of these new trips, 5.1 million will be from suburb to suburb, not from suburb to downtown; and, as the Board of Trade concludes, "building rail transit to facilitate that kind of growth is financially, politically, and conceptually impossible."[52]

Probably twice as many Americans commute from one suburb to another as to the central city. In 1980, 27 million people commuted from suburb to suburb, versus 14 million from suburb to central city. By 1990, more than 35 million were commuting from suburb to suburb, while just over 15 million were traveling from suburb to central city.[53] The new growth communities in the suburbs and in the south, southwest, and northwest are struggling to find an appropriate blend of transportation options.

It will take careful planning to link these smaller, mostly suburban nodes of development with each other on the circumference of the city. Traffic congestion is becoming an increasing bother to peripheral urban areas, and traffic mitigation efforts will intensify as congestion does. Many communities understand that congestion, traffic and aircraft noise, and air pollution diminish their community's desirability. The density of transit-dependent folk needed to make intersuburban travel a reality will increase on the periphery if such trends as reverse commuting and high availability of shopping destinations continue. This suggests that planning must occur now, before congestion overcomes the suburbs more than it already has.

Planning will also recognize the benefits of walking and cycling in peripheral, higher-density neighborhoods, as is done in Europe. In the Netherlands, the bicycle is the second most important form of transportation, after the automobile, accounting for more person-kilometers of travel than trains. The bicycle is used for 8 percent of person-km of travel and 29 percent of all trips.[54] The Netherlands, already the most bicycle-friendly country in the world, adopted a new bicycle master plan in 1992, with the goal of increasing the person-km of bicycle travel by 30 percent over the next 20 years.

It is probably wishful thinking that local governments will attempt to provide disincentives in the future for car travel in an effort to concentrate jobs in clusters instead of having them scattered throughout low-density development—thereby motivating commuters to take mass transit or share rides. This could be tried by raising the tax on gasoline, increasing charges on toll roads, and denying employees subsidized parking unless they use car or van pools. But as Brookings Institution senior fellow Anthony Downs points out in his carefully researched book, *New Visions for Metropolitan America*, such compulsion "is not worth the costs and efforts required."[55] Market-oriented voluntary incentives might have a better result. They would be the opposite of the above disincentives: subsidized parking for employees who share rides, lower state tax rates for businesses that locate in centers where business and commerce already are located, subsidized employer memberships in transportation management associations, and perhaps even reduced property taxes.[56]

So what does the future hold, if the problem in the 21st century will be that urban mass transit has little or no mass? The successful city of the future will not abandon mass transit or less expensive, sustainable, alternatives to more highways and cars. Transit within the city is taking a back seat to transit between suburbs. While the number of commute trips between suburbs is growing significantly, trips from suburb to central city continue to grow as well, albeit at a slower rate. Mass transit solutions need to be addressed at the regional level. Says Dunphy, "abandoning mass transit because commuters to the central city are not growing as fast as commuters between suburbs is akin to shutting off the water supply because your population is declining." Leaders will declare war on congestion. They will probably go down two tracks at once, so to speak, rebuilding old and building new bridges and highways while upgrading mass transit capacity. Dallas has a new light rail system linking the northern and southern parts of the city with the heart. In St. Louis, ridership on the new light rail MetroLink system grew nearly 14 percent in 1996. In Chicago, public support remains strong for that city's superb transportation system. In Los Angeles, the $2 billion Alameda Corridor is taking shape to provide unimpeded rail cargo transport between downtown Los Angeles and the Los Angeles/Long Beach ports, eliminating 200 railroad at-grade crossings in the process at a savings to drivers caught in traffic of about 15,000 hours a day.[57]

Across the country, big-city mayors have been concerned that reductions in federal funding of transportation might impede local efforts to provide transportation for the welfare to work program and transportation alternatives to the automobile for all citizens. They also have feared that the reductions might imperil efforts to repair local infrastructure and improve air quality. Consequently, they lobbied for and applauded the enactment into law of the $215 billion renewal of ISTEA (Intermodal Surface Transportation Efficiency Act) in 1998. "We fought hard . . . [and] now have the opportunity to expand transportation investment all across this nation," said Atlanta mayor Bill Campbell. The core highway program will receive the lion's share of the funds, but the bill also authorized $41.5 billion for transit programs and $1.2 billion for a new clean fuels program to implement less-polluting fuels for buses, trucks, and cars.[58]

A number of alternatives already have been implemented with great success in cities across the country. In Houston, extensive bus and HOV improvements have doubled transit ridership. Eugene, Oregon, is working on "a competitive approach to the automobile." They call it bus rapid transit, a system that would bring together "a variety of proven, low-cost technologies in ways that save time and allow buses to move efficiently through and around traffic congestion." Eugene claims that such a system, with dedicated bus-only lanes to bypass auto traffic congestion, traffic signals that stay green for approaching express buses, and prepaid fares and passes to simplify boarding, could be implemented for about 4 percent of the cost of a comparable light rail transit system.[59]

I hope that rail will be used more for middle-distance hauling in the future—cars for shorter distances, planes for longer ones. Certainly, if there were good rail service between, say, Indianapolis and Chicago, it would be more efficient to travel between downtowns by high-speed train than by airplane. It would cost less and save time. One cannot help but wonder whether or not a lot of old tracks spread across America could be reused to transport commuters to work, especially to downtown locations. By 1910, Indianapolis was being called "The Crossroads of America," with more than 400 interurbans arriving and departing the traction terminal every day, bringing more than 5 million passengers in and out of the city annually, most of them central Indiana farmers and their families.[60] That track is mostly gone now, but could some of it be restored and used to good advantage?

The use of "horizontal elevators," also known as automated guideway systems, will probably become more prominent in the successful city of the 21st century. So far the use of automated guideways, which transport people in elevator-like cars horizontally on an elevated track, has been largely limited to specialized applications, such as airports—and, most recently, at the Getty Museum in Los Angeles. However, some cities, namely Miami, Detroit, and Las Colinas, Texas, have made limited use of horizontal elevators to move people from building to building and to promote downtown circulation. "Intelligent transportation" will become available, linking up drivers, vehicles, and roads in one unitary system. Dependence on fossil-based fuels should decrease in the future as alternative forms of energy, such as gasohol and electricity to power vehicles, are refined and improved. The auto industry, notoriously resistant to these new technologies, is now addressing the problems as well. Zero-emissions legislation in California has forced automakers to focus attention on the development of a viable electric car, and car makers have over the past two decades made remarkable improvements in the fuel efficiency of automobiles. "Smart roads" that use magnets, sensors, and video cameras to help guide cars will be built, like "the nation's first stretch of automated highway that enables computers to do the driving for you," near San Diego.[61]

In sum, the successful city of the future will find alternatives to the automobile by staying committed to maintenance and development of forms of mass transit. It will take nothing short of a cataclysm to convince Americans that public transit should be used as much as it is in Japan and Western Europe, but incremental steps to change behavior can and should be taken.

Transit-Oriented Development

New development and revitalization can be stimulated by planning around transportation. The well-known architect Louis Sullivan coined the aphorism "Form ever follows function" to describe the reason for a building's appearance. When it comes to a city's appearance, the corollary of his theory may be "form ever follows transportation," because throughout history, cities have risen at the busiest intersections of travel and commerce, developing where they had access to ports and navigable and potable water.[62] Transportation—moving goods and commerce and services by land and water and, in this century, by air—has always been one of the chief characteristics of cities.

Where did houses and shops spring up? Where the transportation was. Rather than force communities to fund new roads and bridges and rail systems in order to accommodate low-density sprawl, transit-oriented development (TOD) locates housing and commercial centers along existing transportation corridors. The purpose of TOD is to change development patterns to support existing transportation infrastructure, rather than make capital improvements to support market-based development trends. Linda Morgan, director of the New Jersey office of the Regional Plan Association, says that her state's redevelopment plan "encourages growth where roads, utilities, and transit are in place and discourages it in less developed areas."

The trick is to convince developers, and eventually users (renters, homebuyers, businesses, and retailers) that the market will support TOD. The idea will take root in the future: using a mixed-use transit-oriented village as an organizing principle for creating built, social, and economic environments that not only encourage transit ridership but also foster neighborhood cohesion, promote public safety, and bring vitality to a community by introducing new elements of housing and retailing plus other amenities. The crucial ingredients of these villages are pedestrian access, diversified housing, community safety, and a mix of uses. The concept is enthusiastically endorsed by Michael Bernick and Robert Cervero in their fine book, *Transit Villages in the 21st Century*.

Examples of TOD abound. Along the California Mexican border in the San Ysidro/Otay Mesa zone, development has been so heavy that an intermodal transportation center was planned to get people out of their cars to reduce air pollution. Located at the nexus of rail, bus, and circulator lines, this facility includes a daycare center where parents can safely deposit their children before catching the bus or train to work.[63]

Transit villages will spring up along the BART (Bay Area Rapid Transit) lines in the San Francisco/Oakland area. The Fruitvale Station in Oakland has opened with 67 units of low-income seniors' housing, and an intermodal facility next to the station is under construction. This prototype transit village will include a child care center, senior center, public library, office and retail space, and even a small medical facility. The $100 million cost is being shared by the city, nonprofit agencies, the county, and the federal government.[64] Again, along the western extension into the suburbs of Portland, Oregon's light rail line, city planners are encouraging compact, pedestrian-oriented development around its nine stations. One stop, Orenco Station, has a 190-acre development around it (by the same name), where lots as small as 3,700 square feet and within walking distance of the transit station will be sold. The developer is using a traditional neighborhood design: houses with short setbacks from the tree-lined streets, front porches, and garages tucked in at the back;

pocket parks; and a town center with retail shops and offices. "We wanted to de-emphasize automobiles," says Rudy Kadlub, president of Costa Pacific Homes, which is building 450 houses of 1,200 to 1,500 square feet and about 1,400 apartments. He admits that such a departure from the suburban norm is risky for a developer, but he thinks "the community is accepting it very well."[65] In San Jose, California's Almaden Valley, an interesting prototype development of transit-based housing is being undertaken in a $32 million project called Almaden Lake Village. This new development—the first of its kind—will contain 250 apartments in the parking lot of the light rail station: 200 one-, two-, and three-bedroom units, and 50 units of affordable housing, plus a 150-unit senior housing project. Rod Diridon, executive director of the Mineta Transportation Institute at San Jose State, calls the units "trandominiums." Trandominium advocates hope that similar projects will be initiated on some of the 20 park and ride lots around the county.[66]

Air Transportation

We are moving into the "fast century," as John Kasarda (director of the Kenan Institute of Private Enterprise at the University of North Carolina and senior fellow of the Urban Land Institute) has observed, when international transactions, production flexibility, and speed characterize the new economy.[67] Noting that changes in transportation technology determined America's development—from seaports to rivers and canals, from rails to cars and trucks and highways—Kasarda claims that the key to understanding the current developmental era is to view aviation and airports as "the primary generators of jobs and wealth." He cites three irreversible and complementary business forces as the precipitating factors: the globalization of economic transactions, new manufacturing methods that allow customization and cut production and delivery times, and a growing need for just-in-time logistics.

In the fast century, manufacturers will be required to ship smaller quantities more frequently and more quickly over long distances. Thus, airports, adjacent industrial parks, and free trade zones where the products can be processed will inevitably become important tools of economic development. Here lies an extraordinary opportunity for a city with available land, or possibly a defunct military base. Kasarda himself is working on a cargo airport called Global TransPark in Lenoir County, North Carolina, to prepare that region to meet 21st-century industrial and distribution needs. (International sourcing and sales, and speed of production and delivery, will be critical to competitive success.) This new kind of industrial park, combined with an airport, fuses modern manufacturing and distribution facilities with multimodal transportation, advanced telecommunications, sophisticated materials-handling systems, and state-of-the-art support services. In April 1998, the project suffered a setback when Federal Express decided not to locate its $300 million mid-Atlantic hub at the eastern North Carolina center. But in mid-summer, the complex received a $17.5 million, three-year grant from the Federal Aviation Administration—which means, according to TransPark spokesman Him Sughrue, "the project has turned the corner into the construction phase."[68] Federal Express's main hub in Memphis, Tennessee, has been a boon for that region. For each job at Federal Express, an additional 2.75 jobs were generated in the Memphis regional economy.[69] An air cargo hub also can lengthen the shipping day enough to give a geographic advantage to firms in that area that rely on air cargo.

Infrastructure

Any city that wants to stay competitive in the 21st century will have to invest in job training, education, and infrastructure—the keys to urban economic development, because they enhance productivity. Let's look briefly at infrastructure. *America's Real Estate,* published by the Urban Land Institute in 1997, sounds an alarm that anyone interested in the challenges facing public policy makers should heed. Reams have been written about our country's crumbling infrastructure, but this book documents the problem very succinctly. It points out that because of the drop-off in infrastructure construction over the past two decades, the country must rely primarily on aging infrastructure. "With the exception of state and local water systems, the average age of our highways, streets, telephone and telegraphy structures is higher today than at any time since the start of the Korean Conflict."[70] The federal government classifies more than half of arterial and collector roads in the United States as being in poor to fair condition, and more than one-third of major urban road mileage as congested. Over one-fourth of all bridges are 50 years old or older; one-third are structurally deficient or functionally obsolete. About 2,000 dams are rated unsafe or in need of repair. Capital improvements needed for drinking water systems now exceed $150 billion. Meeting Clean Water Act requirements will take $137 billion and more than 3,300 new wastewater treatment facilities by the year 2012.[71] Aging public buildings, such as hospitals, libraries, recreational facilities, city halls, and courthouses, will be expensive to modernize. The American Public Works Association, an international association of individuals and public and private agencies and companies dedicated to providing high-quality public works services to the communities they serve, is strongly supporting an initiative known as the Rebuild America Coalition (RAC) to draw attention to this problem and find increased funding to solve it. RAC uses the figure of $853 billion to describe the magnitude of the nation's infrastructure repair and maintenance problems.

New York University recently received a $5 million, five-year grant from the National Science Foundation for the creation of the Institute for Civil Infrastructure Systems. Other Institute partners include Cornell University, Polytechnic University of New York, and the University of Southern California. According to Priscilla Nelson, acting senior coordinating engineer for NSF, the Institute will "seek solutions to the problems of age, neglect, and misuse that currently beset the nation's urban infrastructure systems" and will help cities reinvent how they plan, implement, and evaluate those systems. The focus will be on highways, bridges, and water and sewer systems.[72]

Aggravating the problem is the fact that most elected officials and candidates are scared to death of the issue. They fear that discussing it will trap them into advocating a tax increase, a third rail they want to avoid. Regardless, the problem is not going to disappear. The cityship challenge for responsible civic leaders is to build support networks in their local communities to help elected officials make tough decisions about infrastructure spending. If not encouraged, these officials will likely leave it to the next guy. Property taxes alone will not be able to provide the funding needed to rebuild (and build) our country's bridges, roads, water and sewer systems, highways, airports, schools, and mass transit systems. Other methods of financing will have to be found, be they revenue or general obligation bonds, refinancing of existing debt, user fees, development fees—or perhaps most of all, state and federal assistance.

Just before I left office in 1991, the Indianapolis Chamber of Commerce undertook an exhaustive study of our city's infrastructure and came up with their GIFT Report (Getting Indianapolis Fit for Tomorrow). The price tag for repairs, maintenance, and new capital investment was over $1 billion. This was a pretty large order to leave to my successor, but he claims to have had much success without raising taxes by cutting costs, increasing quality, freeing up operating dollars to reinvest in critical infrastructure problems, refinancing existing city debt, and borrowing against "the real, established annual savings from competition," that is, from putting out to bid and privatizing things like the wastewater treatment plant, the airport, street resurfacing, and about 60 other responsibilities of local government. The result? "The largest capital investment program in the history of Indianapolis."[73] Successful cities will figure out how to finance their infrastructure needs without putting the whole burden on the back of the taxpayer.

The Environment

In the 27 years since Earth Day was first observed, considerable progress has been made in the protection of our natural resources. Noted environmentalist Gregg Easterbrook has stated that "America's air and water are getting cleaner, forests are expanding, and many other environmental indicators are on the upswing." He contends that "in both the United States and Europe, environmental trends are, for the most part, positive; and environmental regulations, far from being burdensome and expensive, have proved to be strikingly effective, have cost less than was anticipated, and have made the economies of the countries that have put them into effect stronger, not weaker."[74] Easterbrook's reasons for optimism are illuminating:

■ Twenty-five years ago, only a third of the bodies of water in America were safe for fishing and swimming; today, almost two-thirds are.

■ Smog has declined by about a third.

■ Emissions of chlorofluorocarbons, which deplete the ozone layer, have sta-bilized (although global warming is gradually but emphatically occurring).

■ The cost to electric utilities and their customers to reduce annual emis-sions of acid rain pollutants has been far less than anticipated.

■ Between 1970 and 1995, airborne levels of lead declined 98 percent na-tionwide; annual emissions of carbon monoxide were down 24 percent; and emissions of sulfur dioxide, the chief cause of acid rain, fell by 30 percent.

■ Recycling is no longer a fringe idea. The amount of household trash dumped in landfills is diminishing, and even sludge is being given new uses, such as for fertilizer.

■ The acreage that America holds for preservation has risen steadily.

■ Because of tight regulation and industrial liability, the creation of new toxic dumps has nearly stopped and is unlikely ever to resume.

■ In 1995, only 30 tons of dioxin was emitted by all known U.S. sources combined, suggesting that that problem has been brought under control.

■ Renewable power sources, such as solar and wind power, are being har-nessed, and may someday replace our dependence on fossil fuels.

■ Environmentalism is becoming a core American value. While a majority agreed in a recent poll that "government regulation of business usually does more harm than good," 78 percent of the same respondents also think that "this country should do whatever it takes to protect the environment."

Interest in protecting natural resources and the human habitat, and in fending off the community-killing symptoms of "bad sprawl," is on the wax, not the wane. As in many matters, a balanced approach between doing noth-ing and overreaching seems prudent. While each community must fashion its own approach to cleaning the air and water and preserving green space and ecosystems, collaboration among business, government, and citizenry will help most. There are a number of ways in which a community's com-mitment to enhancing the environment can be made.

Sustainable Development Can Be Encouraged

A city can give sustainability higher priority by encouraging the design of "green" office buildings that incorporate safe or recycled materials (have you ever seen the benches in supermarkets made from recycled paper?); energy-efficient technology; natural and indirect lighting; personal environment managers that let workers adjust temperature, fresh air, and ambient noise in their own cubicles; and much more. Susan Maxman, former president of the AIA and an award-winning Philadelphia architect whose firm specializes in sustainable development, talks about the need for all of us "to tread more lightly on this earth." Pointing to the old Native American adage, "We do not inherit the land from our ancestors, we borrow it from our children," Maxman and her partners pledge to design "in a way that conserves rather than consumes, supports rather than destroys, and mitigates rather than exacerbates the impact of man on the natural environment."[75] Maxman cites the animal shelter she designed for the Women's Humane Society in Bensalem, Pennsylvania (lower Bucks County), as a case in point. Much of the 11-acre site was declared off bounds for development in order to preserve wetland habitat and to avoid building on poor soil or near a power line. Inside, floor tiles fabricated from glass manufacturing byproducts, rubber floor mats made of recycled tires, benches and bathroom partitions composed of 65 percent recycled plastics, increased use of natural light, carpets that use low-VOC adhesive, and T-8 and fluorescent lamps instead of incandescent ones, were incorporated into the building—and a $40,000 annual savings in energy costs has been the payoff.[76]

One developer leading the way in the practice of sustainability is the Durst Organization, headed by president Douglas Durst. He and vice president Jonathan Durst say that "being environmentally responsible is part of [our] personal and business philosophy."[77] They are consequently trying to establish "green credentials" for their project at 4 Times Square in New York. The Dursts admit "there isn't much hard demand for green office space right now," but they see their company as "leading the market" rather than responding to market forces. In their construction process, recyclable and nontoxic packaging materials are being used as well as modular, prefabricated, or preassembled building systems to minimize construction waste. Department of Energy energy-simulation software is helping the team of engineers and environmental consultants design the HVAC and lighting systems as well as the exterior cladding materials and techniques. In the finished building, solar energy will be generated, sensors will turn lights on only when someone is in a room, fresh air will be supplied through a state-of-the-art filtration system, and materials used in the project "will emit few, if any, volatile organic compounds."[78] Energy-efficient computers, printers, and copiers have been specified for the building to create further savings. Bruce Fowle, from the architectural firm designing 4 Times Square, anticipates a 15 percent increase in productivity for workers in the large law firm and in the Condé Nast publishing offices who will occupy 80 percent of the building. He asserts that the benefits of such a "green" building include "reducing energy consumption, minimizing damage to the environment, and developing workplaces in which people are healthier and more productive."[79]

Local governments need to rethink how they approve projects, and they should be willing to engage developers in seeking out and approving alternative development patterns that address these issues. Development usually follows the path of least resistance. Zoning codes that allow and even encourage sprawl will result in that type of development pattern. To encourage sustainable development, cities need to amend their zoning to make sprawl development difficult to obtain approval for, while making more sustainable development easier to approve. While sustainable architecture and development may not be less expensive than the traditional counterpart in the short run, over the long haul they save owners and tenants money. As Americans become more environmentally aware and more determined to practice an ethic of conservation, architects and developers will be moving in this direction.

The Impact of Land Use on the Environment Must Be Stressed

Henry Richmond, chairman of the Portland-based National Growth Management Leadership Project, says that "sprawl has become public enemy number-one." He believes it must be defined as an environmental issue as well as a corrosive cultural problem. James Howard Kunstler, who has a way with words, describes the "junk that we've smeared all over the landscape"—bad sprawl—as "an environmental calamity" and suggests a "restoration of synergistic density, within reasonable limits," based on the model of the traditional American town: smaller lots, more compactness, narrower residential streets, mixed-income neighborhoods with well-defined edges and a focused center.[80] Keith Schneider, former national environmental correspondent for the *New York Times* and current executive director of the Michigan Land Use Institute, claims that "at the grass roots, curtailing sprawl is becoming a central organizing principle for addressing the vexing environmental and social problems that for too long have been regarded as unsolvable."[81]

Waterways and Abandoned Rail Lines Can Give New Life to the City

Many waterways throughout America have contributed to the revitalization of cities because they have been turned into attractive amenities, featuring beautiful waterfront developments, biking and hiking trails, wooded areas, and parks for picnicking and recreation. Look at Cincinnati; Rochester, New York; Sacramento, California; Memphis, Tennessee; Philadelphia; and Miami; these are just a handful of cities that have used their downtown riverfront locations for entertainment and retail activities. In Cleveland, Ohio, empty, derelict warehouses along the Cuyahoga River have been converted into a dynamic entertainment district with more than 40 popular nightspots; North Coast Harbor, a $1 billion, 176-acre entertainment center, has been developed along the lakefront, housing such attractions as the Steamship Museum, the Rock and Roll Hall of Fame, and the Great Lakes Science Center. Chicago, which has cleaned up its river and reversed its course, plans to build a greenway, riverwalk, and high-quality development alongside it.

In addition to waterways, abandoned rail lines can be put to good use as greenways, bikeways, and walkways. Cities can implement a rails-to-trails program that takes up the track and turns the land back to nature. When the CSX abandoned its Monon Railroad tracks in Indianapolis, the city converted the right-of-way into 11 miles of asphalt for walking, biking, and skating. Some unofficial estimates have as many as 500 people per hour using the trail.

Cities Can Plan for Conservation

This means a couple of things. First, cities can plan for the conservation of natural resources, air, water, and land. While I was mayor, concern about air pollution in Indianapolis prompted us to pave dirt alleys and parking lots in order to reduce the number of fugitive dust particles. Since the state legislature was not interested in mandating vehicle emissions testing, which would have helped the city clean up air quality diminished by 100,000 tailpipes a day commuting into its boundaries from the suburbs, the city initiated a voluntary program of emissions testing with companies that ran big fleets of cars. With the help of the federal and state governments, Indianapolis built a tertiary wastewater treatment plant in the late 1970s, making the treated wastewater discharged into the White River more than 98 percent clean. With support and advice from local environmental organizations, the city also constructed a resource recovery facility in a joint venture with the Ogden Corporation to help dispose of the 2,200 tons of trash picked up each day. The trash is incinerated to generate steam, which is sold to the Power and Light Company, and the residual ash, about 10 percent of the original volume, is buried in landfill. We do not need more sanitary landfills in this country. Land is too precious. We need to develop alternatives to landfilling as a way of disposing of solid waste, such as resource recovery, recycling, and composting. Good cityship requires that a large city take a multifaceted approach.

Second, cities can plan for preserving the natural environment. A number of studies have suggested that a city—indeed, a region—can plan to protect habitat rather than give carte blanche to the bulldozer. In March 1996, the final report of the National Wildlife Conservation/Economic Development Dialogue, chaired by Douglas Porter, president of the Growth Management Institute and ULI fellow, outlined several important steps that need to be followed by cities seeking to actively practice conservation.[82]

One step calls on cities to be proactive. Conservation does not just happen. It requires regional planning that initially recognizes and provides for impact on wildlife and biodiversity in the urban region. The development of such a plan can often be stalled by the permitting process. It took more than eight years, for example, for Riverside County, California, to develop a habitat conservation plan for the Stephens kangaroo rat. A delay like this is surely incompatible with the goal of governmental efficiency and effectiveness, and the successful city of the future will streamline its operation to reduce protracted permitting and zoning processes.

Second, funding for the plan must come from diverse sources. Possibly a non–interest bearing loan, a grant from the federal or state government (Florida provides for habitat acquisition funding through its conservation and recreational lands program), or local bonds could be used. Land identified while it is still rural and undeveloped is generally much cheaper to acquire. As an area develops and becomes more urban, land prices rise. Typically, when new development begins to take place in a region the threats to biodiversity are initially ignored or are not immediately perceived. As development continues and the threats become apparent, regulatory responses—such as proposing that indigenous species be listed under the Endangered Species Act—disrupt the economic development of the area, make new development uncertain, and as a result drive up the cost of developable land. These higher costs are then disproportionately borne by new development. The price of waiting until land has become urbanized to implement conservation plans also can be driven up because of fragmented ownership, which is normally less prevalent in as-yet undeveloped areas. Establishing a fund would also protect the rights of property owners by ensuring fair compensation in exchange for placing their land in conservation.[83]

Third, early planning and orderly funding facilitate the accomplishment of the goal. Ordinarily, the longer it takes to acquire habitat, the more disruptive and costly the process becomes. If it drags on, the developer and homeowner are required to bear an unfair burden of the cost. The costs of having to retrofit a conservation plan into a land use plan are quite high, as are the costs of redesigning or rebuilding infrastructure that already has been partially constructed.

Cities Can Commit to "Smart Growth"

Smart growth is an emerging concept that promotes a middle course between no-growth and unlimited low-density land development. It is not a code word either for slow growth or for growth boundaries. It means what it says: growth is inevitable, so let's grow smart—that is, sensibly and sensitively. Smart growth tries to use existing development and make it more environmentally sound and user-friendly. It often promotes higher densities, thereby helping the economy to prosper; encourages greater efficiency and effectiveness in local land regulation practices; and opposes destructive development patterns. Governor Parris Glendening of Maryland has made smart growth a centerpiece of his administration, saying, "the goal is sensible growth that balances our need for jobs and economic development with our desire to save our natural environment before it is forever lost." In Chicago, the Metropolitan Planning Council is promoting the idea of sensible growth as a means of increasing livability in that city and its suburbs.

Cities and states can help to make local sustainable development more feasible and desirable. Cities can rethink zoning laws that require wide streets and isolated uses, for example. At the regional level, cities can band together to identify places that ought to be preserved so that regional ecosystems can be sustained, as Portland, Oregon, sought to do when it implemented growth boundaries. If states were more generous in supplying local governments with annexation powers, it not only would help to widen the tax base and deconcentrate poverty but also would make conservation of greenfields and open spaces easier.[84] States could also mandate the implementation of such a regional strategy—or, using the carrot instead of the stick, make certain state grants contingent upon this kind of planning.

The obsolescence of most standard planning and zoning codes has become a source of considerable concern as we approach a new century. For the most part, the codes were written a long time ago, 50 years and more, which means that many states and cities rely on a legislative framework created for a very different America. The result, as attorney J. William Futrell, president of the Environmental Law Institute, explains, is that "their planning, growth management, and urban revitalization mechanisms are woefully out of step with the times. These planning laws look back to a vanished world, in which planners could not conceive of a society dominated by the automobile, riven by racially divided central cities, losing valuable farmland to suburban sprawl, and smarting from air pollutants transported from a thousand miles away."[85] Developers and other land use professionals should pitch in where they live and work to get these codes modernized or eliminated so that smarter growth can occur.

Brownfields Can Be Cleaned Up and Recycled

A recent survey by the U.S. Conference of Mayors showed that in 122 cities there are 47,000 acres of brownfields spread across 16,500 mostly urban sites. Brownfields, in contrast to greenfields, are parcels of abandoned or contaminated land, usually found in urban settings. Mayor Paul Helmke of Ft. Wayne, Indiana, calls them "dead zones within our cities that should be recycled and returned to productive economic use." Investors and developers may not want to become involved, because the land may be contaminated— but even land that's not contaminated can suffer the same stigma, simply from being abandoned.

The good news is that prospects for brownfield redevelopment are getting brighter. Mayors surveyed by the U.S. Conference of Mayors estimate that a cleanup of these sites could produce as much as a half billion dollars for the yearly tax ledgers of some 100 cities and generate an estimated 236,000 jobs in the process.[86] HUD has twice as much money committed to brownfields in the current budget as in last year's budget.[87] Across the country, brownfields consortiums are pulling together public, nonprofit, and private-sector leaders to assess the extent of the problem and work through it.

Government agencies, which once placed brownfield liability costs on owners regardless of their culpability, are beginning to guarantee purchasers of contaminated property that they will not be subject to future liability concerns, thereby improving the marketability of these sites. In Wisconsin, Public Law 453 provides environmental liability protection to subsequent purchasers of affected properties. The city of Kenosha owns a huge brownfield tract in the middle of its downtown on its beautiful shoreline, and without the help of PL 453, nothing ever could have been done with it. Chicago has an excellent brownfields remediation program, making it clear that redevelopment of polluted properties is financially feasible and environmentally desirable. In 1996, for example, Mayor Daley announced a $50 million program to redevelop 200 acres of brownfields on Chicago's South Side.

A Local Municipal Environmental Court Can Be Established

Indianapolis established the country's first municipal environmental court in 1978. Today, there are about 25 around the nation. The dockets of these courts are reserved exclusively for violations of local health, safety, housing, building, fire, solid waste, junked automobile, and weed and litter ordinances, because in criminal and civil justice systems, such cases are often placed on the back burner. With more intense prosecution of violations, there is greater compliance with local laws, resulting in a safer and cleaner community. Of course, some in the land use industry feel that such a court would be just another bureaucratic bother they would have to endure. But in the communities where the courts have been established (with criminal as well as civil powers to levy heavy fines and have violators arrested and even thrown in jail), they seem to have helped solve urban problems relating to unsafe buildings, litter, rats, contaminated food, substandard housing, fire regulation infractions, defective plumbing, zoning code violations, wildlife issues, and public nuisances.

The most effective court, in my opinion, is presided over by Judge Larry Potter in Memphis, Tennessee. Founded in 1982 and upgraded in 1991 to countywide status (from a limited municipal court), the "rat court," as it has been dubbed, deals with everything from food poisoning to fire-related deaths and rat bites to illegal dumping. Judge Potter actually makes personal inspections of the places his court cites for code violations. In 1994, Potter created an E Team (Environmental Team), composed of inspectors from the housing, fire, health, and code enforcement agencies, to investigate sites of reported or possible code violations. The E Team has been successful: In a five-month period before it was founded, 239 individual cases were brought to the court; in the same period a year later, that number had jumped to 313.

These courts can be helpful to a community, and more should have them. The Keep America Beautiful program, a national nonprofit public education organization with 500 local affiliates dedicated to improving waste-handling practices at the community level and preserving the natural beauty and environment of America, is willing to work with local leadership, "wherever, whenever," to initiate the steps necessary to start such a court.

Government Regulators Can Work with the Private Sector to Make Sure That Protecting the Environment Does Not Impede Economic Growth

Michael Pawlukiewicz, former assistant manager for environmental policy in Prince George's County, Maryland, and director of environmental land use policy at the Urban Land Institute, specializes in smart growth and environmental issues. He feels that the traditional regulatory approach of setting national environmental standards for every state and locality to meet was useful when our country needed to address the pressing environmental problems that existed in the 1970s and 1980s. Now, however, the nature of the environmental problems that confront us do not lend themselves to one-size-fits-all centralized regulation. In addressing the problem of excessive nitrogen caused by storm water runoff in the Chesapeake Bay, for example, it makes little sense to adopt national policies that require enforcement in areas of the country where the problem may not exist. Pawlukiewicz contends that to continue our pattern of environmental improvement and also guard our economic well-being, problems must be managed at the local level, using locally derived solutions. To be effective, these solutions must integrate environment, economy, and community.

Local ecosystems, economics, culture, and history all make each region in our country unique, and because of this they deserve individualized attention. Solutions to today's environmental problems are sophisticated, expensive, and difficult to implement. To solve them, we need to work in an atmosphere of cooperation, not hostility. Regulators should no longer have the luxury of mandating disruptive practices, ordering local spending priorities, and treating committed local officials like lawbreakers when they try, faithfully, to balance complex local issues. I well remember a time when I was in Congress in the early 1970s, and the EPA was threatening to close down vehicular traffic in the Indianapolis downtown business district. I took the floor and exclaimed: "EPA must not be allowed to crucify local business on the altar of federal regulations." Of course, the attainment of clean air and clean water standards is important, but so is local commerce. Perhaps if regulators sought to work more closely with the business community and its representatives, the confrontations that occur as a result of hammer-and-gorilla tactics could be avoided. The federal government should rely less on punitive threats and try to use penalties more judiciously in the decision-making process, seeking to work with local governments as a partner in implementing policies.

For economic and market considerations to be fully and effectively integrated, the business community and state and federal regulators must together participate in the development of local plans, programs, and priorities. Many local officials realize the importance of involving the private sector but have not been successful at engaging business interests in the process. This is one of the challenges facing 21st-century cities. Successful cities of the future will adopt an individualized, local approach, understanding that our environmental efforts must now focus on protecting our natural resources *and* on ensuring our economic growth and well-being.

THUS, THE FIFTH COMPONENT OF MY VISION: THE SUCCESSFUL CITY OF THE 21ST CENTURY WILL DELIVER SERVICES EFFICIENTLY AND COPE EFFECTIVELY WITH URBAN PROBLEMS SUCH AS SECURITY, EDUCATION, HOUSING, TRANSPORTATION, INFRASTRUCTURE, AND ENVIRONMENTAL DEGRADATION.

CREATING "PLACES WORTHY OF OUR AFFECTION"

THE SUCCESSFUL CITY OF THE FUTURE WILL HAVE A VIBRANT CENTRAL CITY, LIMIT "BAD" SPRAWL, AND PROMOTE SMART GROWTH

WHEN I SPOKE AT A ULI district council meeting in Sacramento, I was asked why I used the phrase "bad sprawl," which implies that there is such a thing as "good sprawl." Well, there certainly isn't, if the word "sprawl" is used pejoratively. But if it can be interpreted as "growth," then there are good and bad kinds of growth, healthy and unhealthy. "It is within our power," explains author James Howard Kunstler, "to create places worthy of our affection."[1] That must be the aim of cityship.

Bad Sprawl

Certainly, one alternative for the city of the future is allowing the development of low-density, "bad" sprawl to continue: the endless sameness of structures lacking distinctive form or character; "blobs distending in every direction";[2] cookie-cutter subdivisions and strip malls connected by six-, eight-, and ten-lane roads leapfrogging over each other and gobbling up precious land in the process—all of it accompanied by air, water, and ground pollution, abandoned buildings, smog, and low-density, single-use patterns of development, unrelieved by open spaces or friendly amenities. Bad sprawl lays bare the haphazard nature of unplanned land use. Can't we see it in our mind's eye? Crowded highways and huge parking lots; big-box stores and homogenous buildings; row upon row of monolithic housing; no walkable streets.

The costs of sprawl are considerable. How else can we explain the results of a recent poll conducted in Maryland by the Conservation Fund, a national land conservation organization, in which 84 percent of respondents expressed concern about sprawl, 91 percent said they were worried about the high infrastructure cost of unplanned growth, and 87 percent said they would support new road, sewer, and other suburban construction *only* if it occurred in designated growth areas?[3] Most planners feel that unhealthy growth—that is to say, bad sprawl—is undesirable, and they are asking policy questions aimed at reining in unlimited, uninhibited, untrammeled development. Are there alternative growth patterns? And, if so, how do we initiate and implement them? Is all development good? Where should growth be allowed, and where should it be prevented? What about property rights? How can citizen support for planned growth be created if it's not in place already? Can the brakes be put on bad sprawl without adopting a no-growth policy?

After World War II, suburbanization took hold and outward growth became the order of the day. Some of it could be labeled good sprawl, because it created housing where the market wanted it. It provided new alternatives to existing outdated and deteriorating residential, industrial, and commercial areas. Large-lot, single-family residential developments and other forms of sprawl are fiscally beneficial to local governments in the short term, providing new tax base and "an efficient distribution of economic activities in both a macro and a micro sense. Firms and people are distributed to localities that minimize individual out-of-pocket costs."[4]

Gradually, though, people awakened to the unfortunate consequences of sprawling development. Escalating concerns about congestion, land consumption, smog, and the hidden costs of extending infrastructure (new schools, sewers, bridges, roads) have prompted more and more people to question the benefit of unlimited low-density growth. Sprawl became pervasive because of any number of policies—zoning regulations that required large lot sizes, mortgage interest deductions, state and federal highway building programs, to name a few—and it was not in all cases good. Some sprawl abetted the formation of a suburban America, largely white and affluent, and an urban America, largely minority and poor; it required extensive outlays of taxpayer funds; it gobbled up land and spoiled the environment; and it made a true sense of community harder to achieve. Bad sprawl has had at least six unfortunate outcomes.

First, bad sprawl contributes to economic polarization. It generates what Neal Peirce calls "a kind of American apartheid." New jobs are created farther out on the periphery in places that are difficult for city dwellers to reach. Minorities find it more difficult to purchase homes the farther they travel from the central city. Taxes and development costs increase to maintain the old infrastructure for those whom sprawl leaves behind. A "giant sucking sound" is created, pulling vitality out of the central city. A desire "to be with one's own kind" causes those who can afford it to vote with their feet for low-density locations. People who can't afford a car get shut out. Just look at any central city and ask: Is it not true, for the most part, that the urban core is peopled with minorities and economically disadvantaged persons, while the suburban fringes have become a magnet for those who are white and afflu-ent? In this way, sprawl leads to social and economic polarization, engender-ing an us-versus-them mentality. Robert W. Burchell, Distinguished Professor at the Center for Urban Policy Research at Rutgers University, describes the result: "The reality of unplanned growth brings about a type of economic triage wherein a finite amount of money is allocated to prepare and access new areas while old areas are left to die. These are the middle-stage signs of a region that is becoming noncompetitive and whose end state is a major loss of economic tenants."[5]

Second, bad sprawl consumes land that has other legitimate purposes, including being left alone! Indianapolis (800,000 population; 400 square miles) has more agricultural land within its boundaries than any other big city in the country. As mayor, I was concerned about greenfields being gob-bled up by sprawling development, perhaps not at the rate of an acre an hour, as is the case in Phoenix, but certainly at a pace that concerned anyone in our community who was interested in preserving greenfields, the ecosystem, and open space. On a national scale, public policies permit 400,000 acres of green space a year to be turned into subdivisions, shopping centers, strip malls, and roadways, which figures out to 45.6 acres every hour every day.[6]

The American Farmland Trust says that the imperiled lands cluster around our major cities. Between 1970 and 1990, the Chicago region grew 4 percent in population, but 46 percent in occupied land area. Figures for other cities tell the same story: in New York, 8 percent and 65 percent; Philadelphia, 4 percent and 32 percent; Seattle, 36 percent and 87 percent; St. Louis (going back to 1950), 35 percent and 87 percent. Neal Peirce writes that in the valleys of central California—America's top agricultural resource, with $13 billion in yearly farm production—population is going to triple between now and 2040, and in that time "[l]ow density sprawl will devour more than 1 million acres of farmland . . . costing taxpayers $29 billion more than the cost of more compact, efficient development."[7]

Third, bad sprawl has hidden costs for taxpayers. In Rochester, New York, city officials announced plans in July 1997 to replace an abandoned auto dealership downtown with a 77-unit, mostly upscale apartment complex. This seemingly was good news. However, a local newspaper noted that the city paid $425,000 for the site but sold it to a developer for $110,000, making clear that "the project will be subsidized by taxpayers. If Greater Rochester weren't awash in suburban sprawl, if we weren't building new housing developments farther and farther out, we wouldn't need to underwrite housing on vacant city land. There'd be enough demand for downtown housing to build it without subsidies."[8] The units will be ready for occupancy in the spring of 1999.

Rutgers University has estimated that the infrastructural repercussions of sprawl—building the roads, sewers, schools, and other public facilities needed to serve the new developments—will cost the state of New Jersey $7 billion to $8 billion over the next 20 years, which comes to about $15,000 to $20,000 per household. In Little Rock, Arkansas, growth through annexation on the western end of the city generated new cumulative net revenue of between $8 million and $9 million over nine years, according to a fiscal impact analysis done by Tischler & Associates of Bethesda, Maryland, in 1992. But commercial disinvestment and housing abandonment in the central city "generated cumulative net costs of $32 million" during the same period.[9]

Fourth, bad sprawl increases traffic congestion and reduces pedestrian access to out-of-home activities. Reid Ewing, associate professor at the College of Engineering and Design at Florida International University, analyzed household travel patterns in a sprawling Florida county and found that "households living in the most accessible locations spend about 40 minutes less per day traveling by vehicle than do households living in the least accessible locations (thus generating hundreds of fewer vehicle hours per year.)"[10] In Middletown, Delaware, local government was worried about the impact of exploding growth on transportation. It instituted a traffic calming process, a "mobility-friendly" design initiative that involves reviewing current standards for transportation and land use; reworking subdivision streets and roads to allow new styles of development, such as pedestrian-oriented, mixed-use, and town-centered projects; and the arranging of parking, sidewalks, bike paths, transit facilities, landscaping, and building locations to make shorter trips easier. Said Alexander Taft, executive director of the Wilmington Area Planning Council: "The 1.7 million auto trips made every day in our region are predicted to grow by 40 percent by 2020. Congestion, suburban sprawl, and infrastructure costs will continue to escalate. If growth continues under the shortcomings of current design standards, travel by means other than the automobile will be nearly impossible."[11]

Fifth, bad sprawl degrades the environment by bulldozing greenspaces and wetlands, thereby destroying biodiversity through habitat fragmentation. It prevents natural groundwater recharge and flood storage and generates air, water, and noise pollution from increased traffic congestion. It consumes land in giant bites: While leading metropolises of the early 20th century covered 100 square miles or so, the new suburban city "routinely encompasses 2,000 to 3,000 square miles."[12] A study by the Center for Urban Policy Research at Rutgers University found that in New Jersey, sprawl consumes two and one half times as much land as compact development and leads to a loss of five times as much environmentally sensitive land.

Most of us have never given a second thought to the California gnat-catcher, a diminutive and rare songbird on the endangered species list, the southern California equivalent of the spotted owl. But its plight (as well as that of other species threatened with extinction) and the measures taken to protect it illustrate the conflict that often occurs between developers and conservationists. The coastal sage scrub habitat of the gnatcatcher extends over 400,000 acres from Los Angeles to the Mexican border. Meanwhile, San Diego

County is growing at the rate of 70,000 new inhabitants per year. So, a clash between two forces arises. On the one hand, builders are only too happy to meet the need for new homes and collect the corresponding economic benefits. (The National Association of Home Builders estimates that housing construction and remodeling account for about 4 percent of the nation's gross domestic product and that 1,000 new homes generate 2,448 jobs in construction and related industries, $79.4 million in wages, and more than $42.5 million in federal, state, and local tax revenues and fees.)[13] On the other hand, those who believe in protecting ecosystems and sustaining biodiversity through multispecies, multi-interest planning for wildlife conservation (which is now mandated by federal law through the Endangered Species Act of 1973) are wholeheartedly opposed to such habitat decimation. The solution lies somewhere in the middle: Both sides should come together with government agencies to work out a plan that all stakeholders can buy.

In California, the state has a Natural Communities Conservation Program that could serve as a model for the rest of the country. It was enacted in 1991, and under its umbrella the three southern California counties of Orange, Riverside, and San Diego are jointly planning in advance for the achievement of two goals: continuing business development *and* habitat preservation. Such rational joint planning yields positive results: Late in 1993, development of a 380-acre site in Fullerton was announced by the Unocal Land and Development Company, conditioned on its agreement to set aside 125 acres of coastal sage scrub for the California gnatcatcher.[14]

Land use in America does not have to squander our greenfields. It is possible to have master-planned communities that preserve environmental assets and protect the ecosystem. The 25,000-acre Woodlands development in suburban Houston designates more than a quarter of the community as forest reserves, parks, lakes, and other open spaces. Spring Island, a 3,000-acre development on the beautiful coast of South Carolina, has declared one-third of the island as a nature reserve.

Finally, the psychological and social costs of sprawl cannot be ignored. Reid Ewing observes that the physical uniformity of sprawl is a source of "environmental deprivation" because it makes it more difficult to have strong "communities of place" where neighbors interact, have a sense of belonging, and have a feeling of responsibility for one another.[15] Sprawl kills the notion of community by breeding isolation and spiritual disconnection. Children, because of their inherent lack of mobility, are often the most disconnected. Explains James Howard Kunstler, author of *Geography of Nowhere*, "children are deprived of a fundamental stage of development" because they "need to learn how to get places by themselves—home from the library, from school to the ballfield, from music lessons to home." Kunstler argues that kids need more than a safe place to ride their bikes. "[They] need shops, and cultural institutions, and they need access to these things without the assistance of the family chauffeur." In suburbia, Kunstler adds, "the only public realm for children is the psychotic principality of television."[16]

America is at a crossroads. Buckminster Fuller called it a choice between "utopia or oblivion." We will either take full advantage of all the opportunities at our disposal to create smart growth—the opposite of bad sprawl—or, failing to do so, will continue to collectively fuel the impoverishment of our quality of life.

Downtown

A recent article in *The Economist* provides some interesting statistics. Unemployment in the 50 largest U.S. cities has fallen by a third over the past four years, to about 6 percent. Rates for serious crime have declined to their lowest in a generation. Citing such cities as New York, Los Angeles, Detroit, and Cleveland, the author believes the question is "not whether America's cities have improved (they have), but whether the improvement can be continued."[17]

One part of this improvement can be attributed to the efforts of many cities to reinforce the urban core as a way of combating bad sprawl. Bridges, schools, civic buildings, parks, open spaces, diverse residential units, and amenities (like urban entertainment districts, restaurants, and sports venues), as well as places of commerce and industry, define the urban form. Also of interest to suburbanites, these places create edges by creating a center. Thus, an important land use public policy would be to encourage urban reinvestment without discouraging suburban investment.

Suburbanization

A discussion of downtown revitalization must begin with the demographic fact that many downtowns have been losing population for years. Cities enjoyed their heyday during the late 19th and early 20th centuries, at the height of the industrial age. Immigrants from overseas and migrants from the South and depressed rural areas flocked to the industrial cities of the Northeast and Midwest, making densities high. But gradually the pace of suburbanization increased, thanks to the automobile and the allure of the suburban mystique, with its promise of open space; attractive single-family dwellings built on large individual lots protected by exclusionary zoning; superior amenities; better education; safer streets; lower tax rates; and ethnic, economic, and social homogeneity. Waves of migration from the central city to the periphery since 1940 resulted in a startling decline in America's urban population (which increased 14 percent in the 1940s but only 0.1 percent in the 1970s), while the suburbs have continued to grow (35.9 percent in the 1940s, 48.6 percent in the 1950s, 26.8 percent in the 1960s, and 18.2 percent in the 1970s).[18] Hartford, Connecticut, lost 11.1 percent of its population from 1990 to 1994; Washington, D.C., 6.5 percent; Providence, Rhode Island, 6.3 percent; Baltimore, 4.5 percent; Detroit, 3.5 percent; Cleveland, 2.5 percent; and on and on. The long-term decline of industrial cities with obsolescing downtowns was paralleled by a long-term burgeoning of suburban living. Between 1970 and 1997, suburban family growth outpaced that of cities by a ratio of 5 to 1.

One recent outgrowth of the suburban trend is the popularity of so-called micropolitan areas, small cities located beyond congested metro areas that offer "city" benefits on a manageable scale.[19] According to Kevin Heubusch, contributing writer for *American Demographics* magazine, "They are large enough to attract jobs, restaurants, diversions, and community organizations, but small enough to sidestep the traffic jams, high crime rates, and high property taxes often associated with heavily urbanized areas." Chances are you'll find one near you—from Mount Vernon, Virginia, to Morgantown, West Virginia; from Ames, Iowa, to Ithaca, New York. One American in 20 lives in such micropolitan areas.

As discussed in Chapter 2, Third Wave technologies have dispersed jobs and made telecommuting possible, thereby rendering downtowns less important. Even though analysis of metropolitan household migration patterns shows that the huge population losses for central cities during the 1960s and 1970s have slowed, the fact remains that the norm in residential migration continues to be from cities toward suburbs, with no dramatic changes expected in the foreseeable future.

However, this does not mean that the suburbs can exist independently of the central city. Downtown supplies the heartbeat for the region. Dennis Judd of the University of Missouri–St. Louis asserts that the "suburbs still owe their status as viable communities to the central city's labor supply and economic markets."[20] Theodore Hershberg of the University of Pennsylvania writes persuasively that "the suburbs have a compelling economic interest in Philadelphia's viability," stating that "ample evidence exists to document the thesis that suburbs surrounding healthy central cities are better off than those surrounding unhealthy ones."[21]

Investing in the Central City

Cities die from the inside out. They are saved the same way. Whether the development of the city be monocentric, concentrated around a large central core, or polycentric, where the core is surrounded by a number of satellite nodes and edge cities, decay will spread outward if left unattended. Consequently, stabilizing and revitalizing the center will be a high priority for successful cities of the future.

Cities perform at least four critical economic functions in metropolitan economies. First, they provide most metropolitan-area jobs, including the best-paying ones, and serve as the nuclei of key industries—offering, as economists have determined, the advantages of agglomeration. Second, the city supports firms and industries located in the suburbs by providing actuarial, banking, auditing, and legal services that are harder to find outside the urban core. Third, cities remain the hub of the metropolitan region's civic life, where the major cultural, educational, medical, athletic, and governmental institutions are located.[22] And fourth, they provide many essential so-called switching functions in transportation and telecommunications. Consequently, downtown revitalization should be a high priority for most local officials. Consider the following reasons for investment in America's downtowns.

Changing demographics offer new opportunities. Lewis Mumford cited four great migrations in America's history: 1) pioneer settlement of the continent; 2) development of farms and cities; 3) migration of the farms to urban areas; and 4) decentralization to the suburbs made possible by the development of new transportation and communication technologies. To which Pres Kaba-coff, the New Orleans developer who specializes in restoring historic buildings, now adds a fifth: the return to the historic central city.

Analysis of metropolitan household migration patterns based on the U.S. Census Bureau's 1980 and 1990 public use microdata samples and more recent Current Population Surveys shows that "the dominant trend in residential movement among most population subgroups is still toward the suburbs" and that "a widespread back-to-the-city movement is not likely in the foreseeable future."[23] Nonetheless, the authors of this study acknowledge two important realities: first, "many higher-income households are moving from the suburbs to their central cities"; and second, major cities are faring well "in attracting nonfamily households of people under age 25."[24]

Another testimonial to the trend toward urban rebound could be drawn from the *1998 Investment Strategy Annual* published by Chicago's LaSalle Advisors Capital Management Inc. Two graphs titled "Back to the City" show that a boost to downtowns will be coming from two directions. Empty-nesters and the "echo" boomers (the twenty-something generation) are finding that urban living fits their lifestyles, thereby heralding a possible "rebirth in the urban residential market." Subsequently, the second boost comes in the form of increasing conversion of Class C office space into residential buildings, hotels, and lofts.[25]

Taking advantage of such demographic changes as Generation X-ers and empty-nesters moving into the central city, cities and developers who expend capital at the front end can show a profit further down the road. In Atlanta, developer Robert Silverman wanted to renovate an old 110,000-square-foot downtown office building. For financing, he went to 32 banks, all of which turned him down. After securing construction financing from a Florida bank, Silverman built loft housing and is now enjoying what he terms an "astonishing" return of over 25 percent annually. He advises others not to "miss the boat on this new market . . . of X-ers (those 20 to 29) who want to live and work downtown and are looking for small, reasonably affordable, private, trendy, loftlike apartments, a haven amidst the action."

Pittsburgh Mayor Tom Murphy is spearheading a program to attract development downtown and to create new middle-class neighborhoods by reclaiming land, rebuilding infrastructure, promoting new zoning regulations, and providing tax incentives. Pittsburgh's goal is to build 6,000 new units of single-family houses, townhouses, and multifamily housing, mostly on sites along the riverfront where the old steel factories used to operate. The Associated Press indicates that the demand for these units is growing nationwide.[26]

While the predominant trend is still toward suburban living, the *Washington Post* recently cited a number of "cities on the rebound" that have slowed down their population losses. Denver; Kansas City; Atlanta; Mobile, Alabama; Yonkers, New York; Salt Lake City; Fort Lauderdale; Rockford, Illinois; Cedar Rapids, Iowa; and Macon, Georgia, are listed as having turned losses from the past decade into gains in the 1990s. Cleveland and Detroit, known in the 1980s as "Rustbelt" cities, have moved from respective losses of 11.9 percent and 14.6 percent in the 1980s to losses of only 1.5 percent and 2.7 percent in the 1990s.[27] Interestingly, even with population decline, Cleveland's central city population "jumped 26 percent, and the price of an average downtown condominium or home grew 21 percent. Plus, downtown employment climbed 5 percent from 1989 to 1996."[28] The *Chicago Sun Times* observed that "in the first quarter [of 1998] Chicago saw 1,048 housing starts, up from 742 in the same period last year," another piece of evidence to support Pres Kabacoff's fifth-wave theory.[29]

Successful cities of the future will take advantage of current demographic trends and bring people back to their downtowns by pursuing at least the following strategies. They will:

■ Encourage mixed-use developments and rehabilitation of older industrial buildings for a combination of high-tech offices and residential condominiums;

■ Attract nontraditional markets—X-ers, childless couples, professionals, singles, empty nesters, lesbians and gays, minorities, home-based entrepreneurs—rather than compete with the suburbs for population;

■ Foster small-business development close to residential neighborhoods, because "corporate downsizing and outsourcing have produced an increasing number of small, high-tech businesses and self-employment opportunities";[30]

■ Target financial incentives, such as housing rehabilitation loans or first time–homebuyer assistance, to encourage socioeconomic diversity and stabilize neighborhoods;

■ Support neighborhood organizations seeking to improve their communities; and

■ Provide resources (public safety, infrastructure, job initiatives, social services) to buttress revitalization and conflict resolution.

We are not adcovating "no growth" as a public policy to rein in bad sprawl, but rather, smart growth—growth in urban centers and older industrial areas waiting for renewal, in mixed-use projects, and in low-density commercial strips that could be redeveloped more intensively. We are talking about a renaissance of urban living throughout the country. Developer Dan McLean's Old Town Square 113-unit project ranks among the top-selling projects in all of Chicagoland. And where is it? Smack in the middle of a formerly blighted, high-crime area in South Chicago. Says McLean of his popular development: "People who move downtown want vibrancy—the restaurants, the museums, the plays. About half of the people downtown commute to jobs in the suburbs. They aren't there to be close to their jobs. They are there strictly for the lifestyle."[31]

Detroit has long been regarded as a symbol of the dismal end point of the industrial era; fixing it would be the ultimate urban turnaround.[32] It's encouraging, then, that Mayor Dennis Archer, sparkplug of the revival, points to some interesting changes within the past three years: over $4.5 billion in private investment; two new sports stadiums in the city; federal empowerment zone and state renaissance zone status, both of which bring major investment incentives; the purchase of the Renaissance Center as the new global headquarters of General Motors; and the addition of three casinos to the entertainment and tourism mix. "This is strong evidence that Detroit has stemmed the decades-long trend of decline," says Archer, "and replaced it with a new trend of growth and opportunity." The *Detroit News* feels inclined to agree: The current wave of investment in the city is unprecedented in the past three decades, the newspaper reports, and "adds up to a $5.5 billion building boom that is transforming neighborhoods from the Grosse Point border to the Cass Corridor to the Ambassador Bridge."[33] *Business Week* adds that "some vital signs are improving: unemployment dropped from 16 percent in 1993 to 9 percent last year, real estate values climbed 10 percent in some neighborhoods, and the crime rate is down 8 percent since 1995."[34]

Cleveland's story parallels Detroit's. During the past seven years, two significant retail centers have opened, four new office towers have been completed, four new hotels have been built, 600 units of new rental housing have come to market, major tourist destination venues have been created, and significant transportation improvements have been made.

Consider, also, the signs of rebirth in the Bronx. *New York Times* columnist Bob Herbert, asserts that there is "a great deal of evidence [in the Bronx] that devastated inner-city neighborhoods can be reborn." Cities can rebound! He cites as an example the work of the nonprofit Aquinas Housing Corporation, which has "reclaimed a neighborhood with fresh housing, services for the homeless and elderly, recreation programs for children, and employment training for able-bodied adults." Herbert suggests that the work of thousands of unheralded groups like Aquinas "is one of the key reasons for the improving health of cities."[35] Throughout the 1960s and 1970s, the South Bronx had become the poster child for urban blight. The area had decayed to such a point that two presidents, Jimmy Carter and Ronald Reagan, felt compelled to visit the devastation. Increased federal funding in the mid-1980s helped local community development corporations (CDCs) create more than 22,000 new housing units by the early 1990s. Still, the community continued to lack other components of a viable neighborhood: shopping, health care, child care, parks, safe streets, and economic development. In 1992, the Comprehensive Community Revitalization Program was launched to address these shortcomings. The CCRP chose to work with five existing CDCs rather than through traditional social work and educational institutions, to capitalize on the trust these organizations already had developed with residents through their housing development activities. The professional planners of the CCRP provide the CDCs with staff funding, seed money, and the technical expertise that these organizations often lack. The CCRP also employs community organizers to promote resident involvement in planning and implementation. One example of the program's success is the establishment of the Mt. Hope Family Practice, born of a partnership between the Mt. Hope Housing Company (a local CDC) and the nonprofit Institute for Urban Family Health. The CDC began by holding community workshops to build awareness about the importance of primary health care. The Family Practice, which was opened in 1995, trains and hires local residents for all appropriate positions.[36]

There are no islands; we're all part of the mainland. "Ultimately . . . the suburbs are deluding themselves if they believe they can simply leave the cities to their fate," warns *The Economist*.[37] The suburbs have a tremendous amount to lose if the central cities collapse. Stated in reverse, suburban values and incomes grow faster if the central city does better. Neal Peirce amplifies: "When a part of a region is allowed to wither, the neighboring communities have to carry it around on their backs, bearing soaring social costs for increased disarray and crime, plus the sheer loss of productivity to the region's economy. Taxes are forced up, economic output down."[38] In the District of Columbia area, the suburbs add another $1.50 in economic performance for every dollar of increased economic activity in the city of Washington.

Suburbanites often feel that they can do just fine without worrying about the central city. I recollect a resident of an affluent Indianapolis suburb bragging that she had not been downtown in 12 years and didn't miss it at all. What she fails to recognize is that the economy of an entire region cannot achieve its full potential without a strong, healthy urban core. She also does not understand that a lot of her neighbors commute downtown for work or entertainment, and are therefore dependent on the central city's infrastructure—like flushing toilets—and services—like fire and police. Nor has she thought through the possibility that decreasing property values resulting from urban disinvestment can lower the value of investment portfolios or pension funds (which just might own some of those downtown buildings) from which she and her family might be benefiting. Central cities and edge cities are interdependent; the bell that tolls for downtown tolls for the suburbs as well.

A return on investment can be realized. Returns on investments are achieved in urban developments in the same way as in the suburbs: by improving and adding value to land to achieve a profit. Securing profitable returns in the city, however, is often more difficult than in the suburbs for a variety of reasons, among them higher land costs, disparate land ownership, uncertain environmental hazards, higher taxes, substandard infrastructure, rigid zoning ordinances, cumbersome and sometimes uncertain permitting processes, and a perception among lenders of higher risk that can make financing difficult. The key for city governments is to be a supportive partner in helping developers to overcome these obstacles.

Local governments can encourage private investment by establishing a planning and regulatory framework that removes barriers, allows for flexibility, and streamlines the permitting and development process. Cities can also target areas for redevelopment by making investments in infrastructure; creating tax-increment financing districts to ready areas for development; remediating environmental problems; and assisting developers in assembling land parcels, providing loan funds, and providing property tax abatements.

Comerica Tower in Detroit represents a successful partnering of public and private interests to develop a new Class A office building in the downtown of a city that some had left for dead. The 1992 building was the first new office completed in the Detroit CBD in more than a decade. The Hines Interests Limited Partnership saw an opportunity to build new Class A space for legal and accounting firms, auto companies, and other tenants interested in maintaining a city address. Although the major portion of financing for the project was secured privately, the city contributed three major components that enhanced the feasibility of the project. Specifically, the city provided a $7 million urban development action grant, a $16 million contribution to the land purchase through its borrowing capacity under Section 108 of the federal Housing and Community Development Act, and a land grant yielding a right-of-way and parking lot valued at $6.7 million. The city also granted a zero-lot-line variance that made possible a pedestrian walkway between the tower and parking garage.

In Portland, Oregon, the development of Pioneer Place, a multiuse revitalization project that includes retail, office, and parking, was made possible through the issuance of $32 million in tax-increment bonds for land assembly, tenant relocation, and a public parking structure. The agreement between the city and the Rouse Company allowed the city to convert its land investment into a limited partnership in the project, thus securing a share of the project's future cash flow.

In Indianapolis, a two-block redevelopment project that took 17 years to plan and build created a new downtown shopping and entertainment center out of abandoned land and buildings. The city acquired the land and prepared the site, but the project did not come together until 20 companies contributed $75 million to close a gap in financing. In exchange, they received an equity position in the Circle Centre project, developed by the Simon Property Group and the city of Indianapolis, as well as a preferred rate of return (8 percent compounded annually). The investors are not just preserving capital; they are making money. They received their first distribution of their return on investment in late-1996, and the project is tracking their forecasts. The revitalization of downtown in other areas has reinforced the investment by surrounding it with more office buildings, hotel rooms, and commercial activity.

ETIs—economically targeted investments—also demonstrate how central-city investments can produce a return for the civic-minded investor. TIAA-CREF has set aside $25 million for ETI investing in homeownership in inner cities. Sound ETIs give investors a unique opportunity to satisfy the twin objectives of financial return and social benefit. After the Los Angeles riots, CALPERS (California Public Employees Retirement System) invested $75 million in new construction in south central Los Angeles.

Increasingly, pensions are investing in ETIs. Housing investments receive the lion's share of pension fund ETI dollars: of the almost $20 billion invested in ETIs by public pension funds, 84 percent has been in housing and other real estate. One ETI study (26 were surveyed) pegged the average annual return at 9.8 percent.[39] ETIs are risky, but smart pension funds would not be making investments like these if they received no returns.

Inner-Ring Suburbs

From University City, Missouri (outside St. Louis), to Hempstead on Long Island, from Upper Darby just beyond west Philadelphia to Chicago's Harvey and Park Forest, aging blue-collar suburbs are fighting a battle against decay. Some are succeeding, some are not. Found mostly in the Northeast (suburbs in other parts of the country continue to grow), these belts of mostly single-family houses built around central cities after World War II have limited pools of manpower and womanpower. They have shrinking and aging populations, shallow pockets and dwindling business opportunities, increasing poverty and proportions of minority residents. Urban ills have crept out from the central city: blight, crime, pollution, and educational systems that white, middle-class students are fleeing. Infrastructure is wearing out, city services are wearing thin. At the boundary line between inner and outer St. Louis County, the communities inside the four-lane thoroughfare known as Lindbergh Boulevard, lost 8 percent of their population during the 1980s and median household income dropped 2.3 percent, to $32,745.[40]

What to do? Some proposals suggest new regional governance arrangements. These recommendations are all highly controversial and unpopular with suburbanites who live farther out. They include:

■ Tax-base sharing (newer, more affluent suburbs contribute to a pool of revenue that is reallocated to core area communities) and restructuring of sales taxes to equalize receipts throughout a region;

■ Urban growth boundaries, as an effort to curtail outward expansion and keep new growth closer to existing communities;

■ A regionwide coordination mechanism to supervise local land use planning, so localities will have to consider the impact of their efforts to benefit themselves at the expense of their neighbor, and rational crossjurisdictional solutions to housing, environmental, traffic, and open space issues; and

■ Scattered-site housing, which disperses housing opportunities for poor, inner-city households throughout an area by providing them with portable housing vouchers and affordable housing in the suburbs.[41]

A more palatable technique binds a number of inner-ring communities together to hold the line on further deterioration, on the assumption that "united we stand, divided we fall." In the close-in Cleveland area, Euclid Mayor Paul Oyaski has given strong support and served as the public spokesperson for the First Tier Consortium, composed of communities like Lakewood, Cleveland Heights, Shaker Heights, and Euclid. Oyaski and his colleagues recognize the threat that sprawl poses for the inner-ring communities and are pressing the State of Ohio to require public participation in the process of sanctioning new development and to stop building new roads and start repairing old ones.[42] The Consortium is terribly concerned about the propensity of the Ohio civil engineers in the Department of Transportation to build, build, build (Oyaski points out that Ohio ranks twice the national average in new highway building) at the expense of maintaining what is already in place. He asks, "Why is it that they can find money to propose a $500 million widening of I-71, but they can't pave Euclid Avenue?"

In Minnesota, the I-35W Coalition, made up of seven suburbs heading north from Minneapolis, first convened in late-1996 to discuss and reevaluate regional issues relating to jobs, housing, economic development, and social services. The Coalition has assembled a GIS (geographic information systems) database that encompasses all 46,000 parcels of land in its 77-square-mile area. This will allow the participants to share information and develop consistent and cooperative land use policies.[43]

Without a state's understanding and commitment, regional planning and zoning will not occur, and sprawl will continue. Glimmerings that state governments are beginning to "get it" do exist. For example, in 1992, New Jersey put in place a plan to focus new development on the state's cities and older suburbs, concurrently limiting new development in rural and outer suburban areas. The plan gives established central areas priority in state funding for infrastructure and capital spending on schools "in an effort to steer private development there."[44] States should consider enacting legislation (assuming votes can be mustered from suburban and rural delegations) to base state aid on fiscal need and such measures as a community's crime rate, age of infrastructure, housing stock, and population. Aid for new infrastructure could be denied if low- and moderate-income housing is obstructed, and certain subsidies (such as tax-increment financing, which takes money off the general county tax rolls and puts it into development) could be limited to inner-ring and central-city areas.

Once again, encouraging business reinvestment in the inner ring, making it both feasible and desirable, can help to mitigate the problems of aging suburbs. This is where the art and practice of cityship come in. William Morrish, a professor of architecture at the University of Minnesota, and his wife, Catherine Brown, a landscape architect, founded the Design Center for American Urban Landscape at the University in Minneapolis to develop strategies to combat first-ring decline. They believe that an approach based on coordinating public policy, town planning, and environmentally responsible design will help to alleviate physical deterioration as well as economic and social problems. They point to the recycling of National Boulevard, a decayed industrial strip in Culver City, California, that Morrish calls "an obsolete big box," as a national model for inner-ring renewal. Over the past ten years, architect Eric Owen Moss and developer Frederick Smith have converted several large factories left empty by the demise of manufacturing in this inner-ring Los Angeles suburb into offices for graphic designers, moviemakers, and other media-related professions. The result? The "fusion of economic renewal, innovative design, and cultural awareness" and the transformation of an aging but major commercial and transit corridor into "a lively boulevard of the information city."[45] In short, new vitality for an old inner-ring community. It can happen!

The inner-ring communities are being pulled between two magnets, the central city and the suburbs. Or better yet, between two forces, one of disinvestment, the other of vitality. Successful cities of the future will not focus exclusively on the suburbs and the central city. They will try to tilt these inner-ring areas toward reinvestment and revitalization, saving them from the ravages of further decay.

Reinforcing the Core: Doughnuts and Cookies

When I was mayor of Indianapolis, I used to say we did not want our city to become a doughnut, with all the development taking place on the periphery and the downtown left decayed and hollow. We wanted it to be a cookie, solid all the way through. "You can't be a suburb of nothing," was my reasoning.

One way to prevent the doughnut effect is for cities to lure business downtown by offering tax abatements, infrastructure improvements, and tourism promotion. Most convention centers are located in downtown areas, and the spillover effect of an increase in visitor traffic can be considerable. Some critics question the wisdom of investing in tourism and convention business, claiming that most jobs produced by the industry are low-paying and do not offer any net economic growth, and that the convention trade involves extra costs to taxpayers for provision of such services as police and fire protection and street maintenance. These arguments sound shaky to me. The convention and tourism industry is a $50 billion business in this country. After Indianapolis expanded its convention center in the early 1980s, there was a 384 percent increase in tourism business by 1990, and more than 6,000 hotel rooms were added to the city's inventory. At the latest count, the industry is adding about $1.6 billion to the economy of the city each year.[46] Need more be said?

When it came time to build a new tennis stadium complex as a permanent home for the U.S. Clay Courts Tennis Championships, the city agreed to participate if the facility were built in a downtown location. If its supporters wanted it out in the suburbs, they would have to build it themselves. It was built downtown, as were a number of other sports facilities and some new housing that took the place of empty lots and abandoned public housing projects.

Another way to build cities like "cookies" is to capitalize on assets already in place. For some underused structures, this may not be a feasible option; the location and market are fixed, making adaptive use untenable. Urban markets teem with viable properties, however, from Class B and C office buildings and suburban office parks to defunct department stores, closed military facilities, and obsolete manufacturing and warehouse sites. The real opportunities "depend on a project sponsor's ability to match the asset's phys-ical potential to a willing market."[47]

A first step in the process is to establish the market—that is, whether or not sufficient local demand exists for potential new uses. Then a little imag-ination must be used to determine how the new use can be fitted into the ex-isting structure. Red tape in local government bureaucracies needs to be cut, and financing has to be arranged. Public incentives must be made readily available to the private sector, because things like tax abatements, HUD grants and loans, low-income housing tax credits, tax-increment financing, zoning regulations, historic preservation easements, environmental cleanup, infra-structure improvements, and flexible application of building code require-ments can bolster a project's economic feasibility. The end result can be so-cially and economically beneficial: new apartments, lofts, and condominiums; new mixed uses, with retail on the ground floor and commercial or residen-tial uses above; new parking spaces; new conference and office space; new parks and greenspaces; and much more. In Indianapolis, an old rubber tire manufacturing plant was converted into a new office building for the Indiana Farm Bureau, and an old theater was saved from the wrecking ball and trans-formed into a new performing arts center with a ballroom on the top floor. None of this would have been accomplished without partnership between the public and private sectors.

Cities can team up with the private sector, coupling political will and financial muscle, to bring new life to downtown through high-quality design. Suisun City, California, offers a case in point. In a 1996 videotape titled "Back from the Brink," released by the American Institute of Architects, Suisun City's downtown is shown as it appeared in the early 1990s, full of pollution and blight. "The worst place to live in the San Francisco area," opined the video's narrator. But the farsighted mayor, James Spering, moved city hall to the wa-terfront in 1989 as an expression of faith in the future of the area. Says Mayor Spering, "It was clear to me we had to help ourselves. We had to devise our own solutions, determine our own destiny. That was the key to our turn-around." Subsequently, the San Francisco Roma Design Group was hired to redesign the central core along the river channel, a grotesquely polluted, blighted old oil site. The design came up with a master-planned mixed-use community consisting of housing, retail, and commercial space, plus public open space. Much has subsequently been built. The financing took the form of city improvements ($10 million) and $58 million in TIF-backed bonds that would benefit from the area's status as a tax-increment financing district. Thus, a sense of place is replacing "no-place" in Suisun City, thanks to community vision coupled with good design.

The next step is crucial: cities must streamline their permitting processes. Developers all over America are concerned about bureaucratic red tape. I know one who quit doing business in Chicago because he grew tired of working his way through an unresponsive maze of public agencies and offices. He went instead to South Bend, Indiana, where he could visit a one-stop planning office and take care of all permitting in a single stroke. The successful city of the future will reduce the regulatory burden it places on the backs of developers. While working to keep taxes down, city governments can simplify the regulatory barriers that impede business development. They can cut red tape, become more client-oriented, and develop consistency in their application of ever-changing rules concerning fire codes, occupancy permits, licensing, and zoning. And, of course, they can provide incentives to development in the form of tax abatements, grants, zoning variances, and written-down land costs. Quite simply put, cities that make it easier to do business with city hall will create opportunities to succeed in the private sector, which is at least one key to economic growth.

Another way cities can turn themselves into "cookies" is to expand their tax base, either through internal growth or by expanding their boundaries. This is not easily done. In Cities Without Suburbs, David Rusk, former mayor of Albuquerque, describes the problem of cities hemmed in by incorporated areas. These areas prevent the expansion of the central city because their boundaries already are established, making their independent incorporated status clear. Cities that cannot expand lack what Rusk calls "elasticity." They cannot grow. They are locked in. Securing the authority to annex such areas would help, but it is probably a pipe dream to expect state legislatures dominated by rural and suburban interests to grant such authority anytime soon.

(An exception is Texas, where the Municipal Annexation Act of 1963 gave home rule cities the power to annex extraterritorial jurisdictions—that is, jurisdictions beyond the big city's boundaries—by ordinary council action without public referenda. Louisville, Kentucky, and Harrisburg, Pennsylvania, enjoy similar powers.)[48] Ordinarily, fear of "big brother" and of being homogenized into the central city with all its perceived problems (one of the chief being higher taxes) would make annexations impossible, although it would be to a city's advantage if it could acquire additional territory to widen its tax base and spread the burden of supporting expensive city services over a broader area.

Consequently, cities will rely on innovative approaches to transform their downtown cores into vibrant centers of community life again. In this process, it may very well be the case, as suggested in the section on urban entertainment districts, that the old central business district will be replaced by a new central social district, in which places of entertainment, dining out, and arts and culture dominate the landscape.

Business Improvement Districts

To attract business downtown, cities can help the private sector create business improvement districts (BIDs). The first BID in the United States appeared in New Orleans in 1975; BIDs today number more than 1,000. BIDs are areas in central cities defined by state and local legislation in which the private sector delivers services for revitalization beyond what the local government can reasonably be expected to provide. Funding is derived from tax assessments collected by the city—essentially "self-help through self-taxation."[49] The supplemental services and capital improvements they deliver involve such things as trash collection, security, landscaping, street furniture, signage, and special lighting. Their goal is to make the city more user-friendly and therefore more business-friendly.

New York City's Bryant Park, behind the public library along 42nd Street, used to be one of Manhattan's most drug-infested areas. In the 1980s, the businesses and properties surrounding the park formed the Bryant Park Restoration Corporation. This BID generates about $.16 per square foot from commercial property owners for a total of about $1.2 million annually to be used for Bryant Park. Using monies generated from the BID, as well as other privately raised revenue, renovation of the park began. Today, thanks to a successful public/private initiative, Bryant Park is a beautifully restored, historic spot, an attraction to people and business. Special lighting, new entrances, private security, an absence of trash on the ground, new food facilities, elaborate floral beds, 1,484 movable chairs, clean public restrooms, and free programs ranging from classical music to jazz concerts to movies all have contributed to the renewed park's popularity. Some of the results of the neighboring businesses' investment in Bryant Park: no more homeless encampments, graffiti, or drug dealing; a precipitous drop in crime (only three felonies in six years); and 5,000 visitors on average during lunch hour.

In Washington, D.C., an effort is currently under way to revitalize the historic downtown (100 or so blocks) with the help of a BID. Planned services include security, sanitation, hospitality "ambassadors," graffiti busters and cleanup teams, and shelter for the homeless. Planners and marketers are hoping that this BID's flashy new restaurants, multiplex cinemas, $175 million sports arena, and themelike diversions will create "a cleaner, safer, more welcoming city for Americans to enjoy and show the world."

BIDs are not a panacea, nor are they an unmitigated blessing. Concerns about the fairness of assessments have been raised by some property owners. They question the formulas for assessment, which in some states are ambiguous. Using a BID's tax base to float a bond issue is quite controversial. While some states specifically deny bonding authority to BIDs in their enabling legislation, others do not. Bonds have been issued by at least two New York City BIDs, but the practice recently has come under scrutiny because of concerns that the city could ultimately become responsible for repayment if a BID were to dissolve. Because BIDs are managed and financed by the private sector, which is free to contract nonunion workers, unionized city employees may feel as though they are being finessed out of jobs. Nevertheless, the beneficial and practical impacts of BIDs are well documented. BIDs produce positive benefits at negligible cost and indirectly influence the flow of revenue to local governments, whether through property or sales taxes. This is due in large part to the fact that commercial centers represent concentrated economic value.

Historic Preservation and Public Buildings

Public officials often look on historic preservationists as obstructionists opposed to progress. Indeed, that can sometimes be the case. But progress need not eradicate our roots. There are examples all over America of creative ways in which historic buildings are being preserved and put to new uses. When we built the Circle Centre Mall in downtown Indianapolis, we preserved the facades of several historic buildings and incorporated them into the new structure. In Detroit, an abandoned World War I–era public library has been rehabilitated with a combination of philanthropic and government resources, transforming a symbol of urban blight into a state-of-the-art child care and family support center. The good news is that things like this are happening all over America.

In the book *Changing Places,* authors Richard Moe and Carter Wilkie offer the case study of Memphis, Tennessee, to describe the relationship between historic preservation and downtown revitalization. They trace the descent of Memphis from "Bluff City" to "Doughnut City," as Beale Street (it was called "the Main Street of Negro America" in 1934 by black business leader George W. Lee) and Main Street shut down, development moved farther out, crime accelerated, the famous Peabody Hotel went bankrupt, a landmarked robber-baron Victorian mansion on Union Street was torn down to make room for a fast-food outlet, and in the space of 20 years (1957 to 1977), 11 urban renewal projects demolished 3,000 structures on more than 560 acres.[50] Entire blocks—indeed, entire neighborhoods—were bulldozed or dynamited by the Memphis Housing Authority, so that "[m]ost of the part of the city that had been built up during the boom years of the 1880s and 1890s was wiped out in the 1960s."[51]

A turnaround began when developers like Jack Belz and Henry Turley, architects like Jack Tucker, real estate attorneys like Mimi Phillips and Charles Newman, and other practitioners of cityship were able to see value in their decimated downtown. Phillips moved her law firm into a restored 1912 building on Cotton Row; Newman successfully argued before the Supreme Court of the United States the cause of a neighborhood group called Citizens to Preserve Overton Park, thus saving green parkland from becoming a concrete expressway; Tucker renovated a three-story brick commercial building that dated from the 1850s and put three condos in it; Belz restored the Peabody Hotel to its former glory (even to the point of reincarnating live ducks in the lobby fountain, a Peabody tradition begun in 1932); and Turley restored the 1924 Cotton Exchange Building on Cotton Row and converted the 1923 Shrine Building into downtown housing.[52] Says Turley: "I think sprawl is destructive. It's easy to sprawl. It's hard to redevelop. Downtown is the one place where the real estate guy can provide a sense of interaction and common ground, a point of commonality, a shared place and shared history. And I never could quite get used to the idea of throwing away a perfectly good city."[53]

Memphis still has a way to go. Its historic core is half empty; Main Street is lined with vacancies. Many more local residents will have to move downtown, rather than just attend events there. But the final chapter has not yet been written, as with most cities in America. Cities can rebound, and historic preservation can help to reverse the centrifugal forces of sprawl and reinforce the centripetal ones that root us once again in community.

A city's omission of historic preservation from its planning agenda produces places lacking in character and substance, devoid of much of a sense of community. Our older central cities are full of roots worth conserving. They are the seat of monumental public architecture that supplies a sense of place and a feeling of connection with our heritage. Think of the Louvre in Paris, the Coliseum in Rome, the Kremlin in Moscow. All are hallmarks meaningful not only to those who live in these cities but also to those outside for whom they crystallize the cities' essence. I well remember the first time I entered the halls of Congress as a newly elected member. I was quite overcome by a sense of history and the aspiration and hope contained in that building. It was a moment of awe and deep reverence.

Historically, great architecture has produced great cities. As long ago as the 5th century B.C., when Pericles gave the Athenians their motto—"Honor the gods. Serve your fellow man. Adorn the city"—our civilization has understood that public buildings can preserve heritage and strengthen feelings of community to enrich a nation and its people. Public buildings and spaces create identity and place. They give people something to remember and admire. Indianapolis has at its heart a 284-foot-high Soldiers and Sailors Monument, erected at the turn of the century to memorialize "Indiana's Silent Victors" who died on fields and seas of conflict. In *Inside USA,* author John Gunther calls it the "second ugliest monument in the world." Not very flattering recognition—but to many Hoosiers, the monument is a centerpiece, a source of pride, a gathering place, a central point where past, present, and future come together in limestone and bronze.

The challenge facing public architecture is to provide every generation with heroic structures that link them with their roots, fill them with pride, and reinforce their sense of belonging. Thoughtful mayors like Joe Riley of Charleston, South Carolina; Victor Ashe of Knoxville, Tennessee; and George Latimer, formerly of St. Paul, Minnesota, believe that the mayor is "the chief architect of the city," who must understand how public design policies can influence for better (or worse!) the urban built environment. Anyone who has ever visited Charleston can certainly see how historic preservation, walkable streetscapes, downtown retail, and housing have come together to form a beautiful, livable city. Ed Feiner, chief architect of the General Services Administration, which operates and maintains federal buildings throughout the country, told a group of mayors and ULI members gathered in Knoxville for a mayors' forum in September 1997, "We decided, back in the late 1980s . . . [to] build a living legacy of the work of our generation of architects and designers within their communities." He pointed to the new million-square-foot federal office building in Oakland, California, as an illustration: a beautiful twin tower building that is fast becoming not only the heart of the new Oakland but also an icon in the Bay Area. (Feiner says he is sure of this because you can buy refrigerator magnets in the shape of this building and see it on the cover of the telephone directory.)[54] He also described the GSA's Good Neighbor program, which not only offers the use of federal spaces for a variety of cultural, recreational, and educational uses but also gives priority consideration to locating new buildings in central business districts and using historic buildings within those areas.

Successful cities "nurture the insight and the courage to be exceptional," according to architect Vernon Swaback of Phoenix.[55] "Heroic structures," he writes in his new book, *Designing the Future,* "are among the highest expressions of human achievement, without which there can be no culture." Many of the new federal courthouses across the country, either completed or under construction, meet this challenge. And one can only wish, in this era of public penny pinching, when so many elected officials adopt a green eyeshade approach to government, that public officials would be willing to spend the dollars necessary to fulfill George Washington's belief that "public buildings in size, form, and elegance must look beyond the present day."

Taxes and Incentives

Keeping a lid on taxes in the central city is another key to preventing the flight of capital and human resources to the city's edge. Obviously, this is easier said than done. The playing field is already uneven. In Indianapolis, a $10 million downtown office building with an estimated assessed value of $2.21 million pays $217,306 in taxes. In a suburban location, the same building would pay only $100,081.[56] No mayor or city council can control the entire downtown tax rate, because the public schools, welfare, and other independent municipal agencies have taxing and bonding powers also. But lower taxes create more opportunities for growth than higher ones. The Cato Institute, a conservative think tank based in Washington, D.C., asserts that raising taxes stifles economic growth. "Cities with high spending and taxes in 1980 lost population in the 1980s; cities with low spending and taxes gained population. High spending and taxes are a cause, not just a consequence, of urban decline."[57]

Incentives like tax abatement, tax-increment financing, writing down the cost of land, and grants and loans can have a positive effect on economic development and ought not be cavalierly dismissed as welfare for the rich.

One school of thought claims that spending money on tax concessions erodes a local government's fiscal capacity to strengthen education and infrastructure and other services essential to an area's economic future. In the

Journal of Urban Affairs, Harold Wolman advises that policies designed to entice business through government-sponsored financial incentives should be abolished. Instead, "state and local governments should seek to strengthen the competitive advantages of their business environments through policies that enhance productivity, such as education, worker training, and infrastructure development."[58]

This camp makes a good point—but in the real world, outside the ivory tower, a city may lose out if it has no incentives to offer for attracting and retaining business. If Indianapolis had not assembled the property, vacated the street, moved a sewer line, and offered tax abatement, the American United Life Company would not have chosen in the late 1970s to relocate to a new 40-story skyscraper in our downtown. Unless Congress levels the playing field among states by mandating certain requirements, such as prohibitions or caps on local subsidies given to businesses to attract or retain them (professional sports offer a good example), or unless states and locals agree among themselves not to compete and ratchet up the bidding against each other, incentives will not disappear.

Incentives do not always mean higher taxes. In the long run, applying the "but for" test—"but for" the incentives, the improvement might not take place—can help gauge how much more money can be generated by a newly developed or redeveloped property made possible through some form of financial assistance. Successful cities will have it both ways: they can try to hold the line on taxes, invest in infrastructure and education, and also provide incentives to attract businesses or entice them to stay.

Urban Enterprise Zones

Enterprise zones, or "empowerment zones" and "enterprise communities," as they were labeled in 1993 federal legislation, are blighted areas, economically distressed and geographically defined. Jack Kemp, former Congressman from western New York and former Secretary of HUD under President Bush, is generally credited with popularizing the idea in our country. By mid-1994, more than 3,000 zones had been established across the United States, stimulating some $40 billion in investment and producing 663,885 new jobs. After the passage of the 1993 federal legislation empowerment zones (six urban, three rural) were created, each one receiving a one-time grant of $100 million, along with 95 enterprise communities (65 urban, 30 rural), with $3 million being granted to each. Created by federal or state government, zones become vehicles for special grants. They provide access to specialized technical worker training and job placement assistance programs, reduce development fees, and involve favorable tax treatment: tax abatement and relief of the inventory tax (in Indiana), for example, as well as tax credits for employee wages and equipment purchases. (One of the things Congress could do to help these zones encourage more business investment would be to provide a break for them on the capital gains tax.) Social services—such as daycare or shelter for the homeless—are often provided in the zones.

The basic idea is to infuse vitality into a devitalized area. This kind of improvement strategy has been described as "gilding the ghetto" and as "ghetto enrichment" by critics who question its effectiveness in integrating minority and low-income people into the mainstream of community life—where there are better neighborhoods, better schools, and better jobs.[59] Certainly, breaking down the barriers that isolate people by race and economic status is difficult at best. Nevertheless, the zones are one strategy to address urban decay, and a marvelous opportunity for a city and state to cooperate. In Evansville, Indiana, 2,300 jobs were lost when a Whirlpool plant closed in 1982. This struck a severe blow to that industrial city on the Ohio River in southwestern Indiana, turning some 2.5 square miles of the urban area into a wasteland. But thanks to the subsequent creation of an enterprise zone by the state, with its attractive feature of 100 percent forgiveness of Indiana's burdensome inventory tax, new investments in the zone have created some 8,000 new jobs, filled 2 million square feet of vacant industrial and commercial space, and given rise to a million square feet of new buildings. The zone includes manufacturing (Red Spot Paint, Johnson Plastics) and distribution facilities (T. J. Maxx has a center there employing 1,400). In San Diego, where two zones were created by the state of California in the mid-1980s, more than $50 million in private investment was stimulated in the first seven years of their operation. More than half of the 2,400 jobs created for low-in-

come, unemployed people went to zone residents, and 300 permit applications for new construction were processed. The Barrio Logan Zone, located
in a more economically challenged, linguistically isolated area of San Diego,
has enjoyed an increase in jobs and tax base, with the help of hiring tax credits provided by the city and a state sales tax credit.

Enterprise zones are not an instant cure for urban decay, but with support and leadership, they can be effective in countering what Senator Joseph
Lieberman (D-Conn.) calls "the one most important cause of urban decline—namely, the reduction of business activity, and therefore [of] investment and jobs."[60]

Smart Growth and Higher Densities

Sprawl is growth and growth is sprawl. Some of it is good, some of it bad.
Bad sprawl pursues unlimited, low-density growth; good sprawl appreciates
the ability of higher densities to conserve land. Bad sprawl tramples on the
environment; good sprawl respects it. Bad sprawl eschews comprehensive
planning; good sprawl embraces planned communities in the suburbs, inner
ring, and downtown. Bad sprawl practices monolithic single-use land use patterns; good sprawl believes in mixed uses and flexibility in the regulatory
process. Bad sprawl leapfrogs; good sprawl proceeds concurrently with public infrastructure and services. Bad sprawl believes that big is better; good
sprawl sees beauty in the small. Bad sprawl forces people into their cars; good
sprawl gets them out. Bad sprawl loves asphalt and concrete; good sprawl
loves green space.

Extensions of metropolitan areas toward their perimeter and beyond
do not necessarily connote something "bad"; suburbanization is not in and
of itself bad. To support smart growth is not to advocate that development
should occur only in the central city. My former colleague at ULI, Tom Black,
has put it this way: "The opponents of sprawl tend to ignore the fact that
sprawl is not an objective that anyone seeks but is instead the cumulative and
combined result of the pursuit of other important objectives, such as better
housing values, less congestion, safety, good schools, cheaper modern in-

dustrial and commercial space, lower taxes, and lower labor costs."[61] The key to good sprawl is to plan the growth, to do it smartly.

One part of growing smart involves creation of higher densities. Density is a relative term: It could mean a few units per acre or several hundred, and it can apply to suburban, infill, and downtown sites. But a trend seems dominant in practically all areas of the country: Densities are increasing.[62]

By high density, I do not mean warehousing people in high rises. Higher density means clustered mixed-use development with good pedestrian access to services and shopping and with convenient transit access to employment, as in Alexandria, Virginia. High density is obviously the opposite of low density—scattered, haphazard development on the urban fringe. Of course, in big cities like New York and Chicago, 80 to 100 units per acre are acceptable; but for new infill development, 12 to 15 units per acre seems to be the norm.[63]

High densities have a bad name. People think they are responsible for crime, decay, smog, blight, and a host of other ills. But what about San Francisco, New York, Chicago, and Boston? They have densities ranging from 80 to 275 dwelling units per net residential acre, and they have the capacity for continual renewal. An analysis of deteriorating communities near these cities shows that the failed neighborhoods are half the density of successful ones in the same metropolitan area.[64]

Picture a declining quasi-industrial neighborhood, first settled in the 17th century, with land along a river bank that had become a scrap metal yard after years of being home to oyster fishermen. Above the 4.5-acre site stands a bunch of historic Victorian homes. The local redevelopment agency holds a design competition, and sells the land to the winner, who develops the site with 88 units, or 20 per acre. The project includes Victorian townhouses, two-story Cape Cods, and triple deckers (two units on each of the three levels in a townhouse-style setting). Construction financing is arranged; when the units are built, they harmonize nicely with the neighborhood's architecture and history, sell at affordable prices ($65,000 to $85,000), and appeal to a market of first-time buyers, singles, and yuppies, who enjoy the convenient access to shopping, churches, restaurants, employment, and public transportation. And what do you have? You have Riverplace, in New Haven, Connecticut, an example of smart growth and higher density in an area ten minutes from downtown.[65]

Higher densities have their benefits. They preserve valuable habitat, recreational areas, and agricultural resources; help curb bad sprawl and reduce the air pollution, traffic congestion, and infrastructure investment that accompany it; benefit taxpayers who have to pay for the hidden costs of bad sprawl; increase land values and make possible the redevelopment of existing buildings and sites; support public transit and neighborhood retail businesses; and produce more revenue for schools and other public services.[66]

In Chicago, they call it "growing sensibly." The city's Metropolitan Planning Council, a broad-based nonprofit organization, has mounted a Campaign for Sensible Growth to demonstrate that in the Chicago region, economic goals are not in conflict with objectives for a healthy environment and livable communities. The campaign has arisen as a result of "concerns . . . over the depletion of land and the efficiency and social consequences of fragmented, low-density development. The cost of this expansion," continues the campaign guidebook, "is hitting the suburban taxpayers as more schools are built, roads are extended, and tolls are collected. People who moved in search of community and open space are finding instead traffic congestion, long commutes to work, and a loss of natural areas." The guidebook, which showcases the best development practices throughout the region, provides a primer for smart growth:

1. Walkable Neighborhoods
- Plan for a network of destinations with paths and sidewalks close to and convenient to homes, stores, offices, train stations, and bus routes;
- Improve the street environment through the use of sidewalks, large trees, and landscaping;
- Reduce speed limits and width of streets in town centers; and
- Place buildings close to the street, and locate parking lots on the side or to the rear of buildings.

2. Housing
- Allow for a variety of housing—single-family, in-law flats, and multifam-

ily—in new developments;

- Mix housing with nearby retail and services, such as daycare;
- Cluster housing near transportation and jobs;
- Plan for protected open space along with housing development; and
- Ensure that housing is available for working families.

3. Retail Development

- Build on the assets of existing suburban downtowns;
- Transform malls into hubs for the community;
- Allow for multiple uses with housing or offices above stores;
- Encourage people to stroll by creating focal points, upgrading streetscapes, and providing welcoming street furniture; and
- Do not zone more big-box or category-killer stores than the market will absorb, and integrate such development into centers (through pooled parking and access to transit) rather than in isolated developments.

4. Office Development

- Plan employment closer and more accessible to housing, services, and retail stores;
- Redevelop commercial centers using existing infrastructure;
- Allow for greater access to commercial districts via public transportation; and
- Maximize use of open land and natural landscaping in building office parks—make them true amenities for workers and nearby communities—and reduce landscape maintenance costs.

5. Environment

- Preserve open space, and thereby reduce stormwater runoff and provide additional filtering of treated wastewater;
- Protect significant natural features, such as rivers, wetlands, and forests;
- Maintain biodiversity by protecting large tracts of land through land banking and siting, rather than isolated pockets for each development; and
- Encourage more compact development around existing sewer and water utilities.[67]

Public Policy Considerations

We need to counteract bad sprawl by developing public policies that will remove barriers to compact urban development. At the federal level, it has been well known for many years that an anti-city bias exists in public spending and the tax codes. For example, highways are funded, but mass transit is shortchanged. Interest on mortgages helps homeowners, but not renters. Nonetheless, these are some changes in attitude.

The General Services Administration, which operates and maintains federal buildings, has a policy of giving first consideration to locating in central cities and historic districts and to rehabbing buildings like courthouses in the urban core, rather than moving to the suburbs or building new offices. GSA Chief Architect Ed Feiner says that the goal is to commit to the city center and build there rather than on the periphery, with the expectation that these federal investments will provide anchors or magnets to attract further development. Perhaps the states will follow suit. A new Maryland bill, for instance, seeks to require all state agencies to locate their offices in downtown areas—not just in Baltimore, but throughout the state.

A recent change in public policy may turn out to be a boon for cities. A 1997 tax bill did away with the housing capital gains tax (up to $500,000) for a married couple. While the law is patently unfair to homeowners who lose money when they sell their house, since the loss is not deductible on a tax return, its benefit to the cities could be significant. Under the old law, federal policy required people to pay a capital gains tax on their gain unless they rolled it over within two years into a new home worth at least as much as the one they sold. Now, sellers can keep their money. The advantage for central cities is that people, most likely empty-nesters, will be able to sell their large suburban pads and buy or rent for a lot less downtown, freeing their profits for investment in other areas.

Governor Parris Glendening of Maryland described his state's far-reaching smart-growth initiative in a recent speech at ULI's Smart Growth Conference: "For the first time, the state said that locally designated growth must meet minimum state criteria for average residential density and the provision of public water and sewer service. If they do not meet the minimum criteria, they will be ineligible for traditional state assistance. Simply put: If homebuilder A is building in a smart-growth area, with water and sewer and adequate density, he or she will get help with tax credits, roads, and other infrastructure improvements. If homebuilder B is building on land outside a designated smart-growth area, that is his or her legal right. But he or she will get no state tax credits, no state help with water and sewer, and no state help with roads."[68] Glendening's idea has vociferous critics, who argue that smart-growth policies constrain their freedom to build, do business, and locate where they want. One Baltimorean responded by saying that the governor was "trying to force business to move back downtown," which is not the case at all. The Maryland smart-growth program allows builders to build wherever they want. There is no constraint on freedom. They just can't have public money to support their project unless they develop where the state wants to invest.

But of course, local government carries most responsibility for the zoning policies that can help to redirect development toward the core. The case for denser, more mixed-use development was stated well by Rick Cole, Nancy Gragaro, and Judy Corbett in the September 1996 issue of *Urban Land:*

> The preference of most developers to build on raw land is less a product of market demand than of costs and opportunities, many of them directly imposed by local government policies. These policies have shifted the economic, social, and environmental costs of sprawl away from developers of raw land to society in general and shifted opportunities away from existing cities toward areas on the urban edge.
>
> Now an increasing number of players in the development arena are rethinking real estate formulas. They are not only promoting reinvestment in existing urban and inner suburban areas but also fostering a rebirth of compact, transit- and pedestrian-oriented developments that conserve energy, enhance air quality, and help restore community vitality. They are challenging more than just the imbalance to developers' pro formas. To promote infill development, they are pushing for fundamental changes in existing zoning codes, local political climates, lending practices, and public perceptions.[69]

Cole, Gragaro, and Corbett suggest a menu of policies to overcome the barriers to achieving a more compact urban form that counteracts bad sprawl.

They identify such public-sector strategies as zoning for mixed-use and higher-density development, assisting with project financing through predevelopment grants and loans, streamlining the permitting and environmental review process (in Indianapolis, this government function has been privatized, with the result that turnaround time has been chopped from four weeks to 4.3 days), encouraging rehabilitation, providing in-kind assistance, addressing toxic contamination, and providing public services.

Public policy makers should read Jane Jacobs's seminal 1961 work, *The Death and Life of Great American Cities,* in which she warned of the dire results of large-scale "cataclysmic" projects that were "sacking" the cities and argued for greater density and diversity. While her highly influential, if controversial, thesis questioned the wisdom of modernist mega-planned development and urban renewal, her ideas are as applicable to the development of suburbs and edge cities as to central cities. She has said that a phone book's yellow pages "tell us the greatest single fact about cities: the great number of parts." Her view is that "commerce is the mark of urbanity," which means that smart growth will create both density and diversity of commercial opportunity—like Tysons Corner, Virginia, and Bethesda, Maryland, in the Washington, D.C., area.[70] Her book is worth reading again today, almost 40 years after she wrote it. She distinguishes between disorganized and organized complexity, suggesting that a city is a process in organized complexity because it contains a sizable number of factors all varying simultaneously and in subtly interconnected ways, interrelated in an organic whole.[71] Well-planned shopping malls that offer a wide array of shops, restaurants, and entertainment, like the one outside the nation's capital in Crystal City, Virginia, offer an example. So do downtown redevelopments, like the conversion of a 1914 department store by DePaul University in Chicago into a thriving multipurpose commercial center of retail, office, academic, and administrative support space.

In an E-mail response to an article I wrote for my ULI Web site that mentioned Jacobs's book, a suburbanite outside of Atlanta writes: "Density and diversity work. The question shouldn't be how we can rebuild our cities, but how are we going to rebuild our suburbs when everyone finds out the quality of life sought is being destroyed by the quality of life seekers. I live outside Atlanta. It is horrible out here. Everywhere looks the same. . . . But there is something happening . . . . Revitalization, in-town living, adaptive reuse . . . . Too bad those who sit on planning and zoning boards haven't heard of Jane Jacobs; they might not be afraid of a little organized complexity." Public policy leaders, take note!

Creating Livability

In a time of high tech and low touch, when people feel isolated behind their computers or inside their gated communities or out and about on their mind-numbing freeways, smart-growth policies can create more vital places to live. Michael Pawlukiewicz, ULI's guru of smart growth, has said that smart growth is "a new concept in land development that recognizes the link between quality of life and development patterns and practices." He continues: "Communities that follow smart-growth principles use the occasion of new growth to improve environmental quality, enhance economic opportunity, and build community." I once heard Marguerite Wilson from Paradise Valley, Arizona, make the following observation at a roundtable discussion about how suburbanization has destroyed the sense of community: "The center of my kids' life now is the mall. In our city of 7,000, there is absolutely no community. You have to drive elsewhere and everywhere to get anything. By contrast, I grew up in a New Jersey town of the same size, but it was heaven as a community. Good housing, religious institutions, recreation, parks, places to congregate, local libraries and schools, restaurants, retail—it had it all. Plus a strong homeowners' association to take care of the common places. But no mall. It was a lot more than just architecture and front porches."

Two of the main ingredients for livable communities are a blend of density and open space. Prairie Crossing, a residential development north of Chicago, is often cited for its careful preservation of the environmental surroundings and harmonized approach to the environment. Its developers call it a conservation community, guided by such principles as environmental protection and enhancement, a healthy lifestyle (it has an indoor fitness center and ten miles of walking trails), a sense of place and community, high design standards, high-quality construction, convenient and efficient transportation, energy conservation, sensible budgeting for long-term success, and occupant diversity. When finished, there will be a maximum of 400 units on 667 acres, but 70 percent of the land will be open space to be shared by the community, a good example of smart-growth planning for natural areas.

Or take a look at the Field of St. Croix project in Lake Elmo, Minnesota, which provides living proof that open space and higher densities are not incompatible. On a 226-acre development originally zoned for ten-acre lots, a rezoned cluster plan gave the project more than 60 percent more permanent open space with four times the density. In an article for *Planning* magazine on Las Vegas, the nation's fastest-growing city, David Clayton has placed the challenge on developers and urban planners everywhere: "The process of transforming the tiny railroad town of a century ago into a sprawling urban center has also brought urban ills, including crime, air pollution, and crowded schools. It falls to city and county planners to fashion a workable society in an arid desert more suitable for rattlesnakes and cactus than suburban lawns."[72] Summerlin, a beautifully planned, mixed-use development on the edge of the city, meets Clayton's challenge, with its development of 20,000 acres that will have a density of about three units per acre and a population of 160,000 to 180,000 when completed.

Livability is not exclusively a suburban phenomenon, by any means. All over the country, livable communities have been springing up in urban areas as well. Every city has a wide range of financial and regulatory resources to stimulate private investment in inner-city neighborhoods—things like low-income housing tax credits, neighborhood development bonds, tax abatement, written-down land costs, utility discounts (Cleveland Public Power discounts some 30 percent of electricity costs for commercial and residential use in parts of the city), community development block grant funds, and housing rehab programs. These tools can be coupled with high-quality design and private-sector know-how to raise countless phoenixes from the ashes of urban decay.

One of the best I have seen is the Quality Hill urban revitalization project in Kansas City, Missouri, which has over 8.5 acres with ten new buildings, 13 historic ones that were renovated, and two above-ground parking structures. It was developed by McCormack Baron & Associates out of St. Louis with a financing package of about $40 million, with contributions from individual members of a limited partnership; a consortium of Kansas City businesses, banks, and foundations; and the city, which came up with $18.5 million, low-interest loans, and tax abatements, plus a federal UDAG (Urban Development Action Grant).

Quality Hill is a good example of how public/private leadership and partnership can transform a deteriorated area (near what used to be the Kansas City stockyards) into a livable, healthy downtown neighborhood, which not only has its own integrity and beauty but also considerable positive economic impact. A stunning collection of red brick buildings with white trim and gray sidings, Quality Hill blends in with the mostly residential roots of the neighborhood but is enhanced with some commercial and retail, pedestrian-friendly, safe and secure spaces, with easy access to the central business district. This magnificent project stimulated the development of 800 to 900 additional housing units and about a million square feet of new or rehabilitated office space. It also became the location of choice for several nonprofit organizations, like the United Way and the Hispanic Economic Development Corporation, thus increasing the downtown employment base.

Growth guidance strategies (I prefer this phrase to growth management, which implies a heavy hand of control from government) can be used to maintain livable communities because they attempt to prevent sprawl. Governor Christine Todd Whitman of New Jersey summarized the notion well in a speech to the Somerset Alliance for the Future. After talking about how easy it is for land that has been pristine for centuries to be consumed by housing developments and office and industrial parks, she said, "I am not against development, and nobody here in this room is against development, but I think we all understand that we have to control it, we have to manage it, and we have to make sure that we contain it so that the ratable chase [New Jersey refers to tax revenues from new projects as "ratables"] doesn't become a drain that takes from all of us our quality of life, but rather that development is something that enhances us and our communities."[73]

Smart growth as a trend is a late–20th century phenomenon, but it's not a fad. It is part of making a successful transition to the 21st century because it provides an antidote to bad sprawl. Other states, in addition to New Jersey, have taken up the cudgels for it. Hawaii has statewide zoning. Maryland Governor Parris Glendening believes that state government and state taxpayers have a "legitimate, justifiable interest in . . . local land use decisions." Florida has a very comprehensive law on its books, the Growth Management Act. (Orange County, for example, relies on an urban services area to cope with the rapid growth around Orlando.) In 1988, Rhode Island adopted legislation requiring local communities to set specific goals in such target areas as land use, housing (including affordable housing), economic development, and open space. Oregon has the oldest and strongest commitment to growth management in the nation, with its famous Urban Growth Boundary (UGB) plan that in essence draws a ring around a city, like Portland, and constrains development to the area inside the line. These plans all have in common what is called the principle of concurrency, which allows development to take place only if it is concurrent with adequate infrastructure and public services. All smart-growth provisions aim at the same thing: preventing urban sprawl by concentrating development within a specific area that has a compact and contiguous form.[74]

Critics of these plans make some valid points. If UGBs can be expanded, they really don't do the trick, because no permanent open space or rural buffer can be established. They can also encourage development to hopscotch over the area to an adjacent county that does not have similar restrictions (Orange County, Florida, discovered this). In 1994, an appellate court ruling struck down Oceanside, California's annual numerical limit on housing units as "being in conflict with state housing and planning law," thus calling into question the legality of all such caps.[75] Again, UGBs can have unfortunate unintended consequences, such as the displacement of residents in redeveloped areas who cannot afford new housing, an increase in traffic congestion and housing prices, the failure of new parkland to keep pace with population growth, and the birth of interest groups organized for the sole purpose of opposing boundary changes.[76]

These criticisms all are on point, but if all possible objections to a project were first removed, nothing would ever be accomplished. With responsible zoning and planning, UGBs can help to counter the haphazard development patterns of bad sprawl and ensure a higher quality of life. They will constitute one arrow in the quiver belonging to cities that understand the importance of sound growth guidance.

Compact Urban Form

As America becomes more aware of the consequences of bad sprawl, an effort is being made to promote a more compact urban form. Let's look briefly at three examples.

In Bloomington, Indiana, a city of 60,000 people, a tremendous controversy erupted in July 1997 over whether or not to approve a doctor's plan to develop a huge tract of land he owns on the edge of this medium-sized city. Bloomington's growth policies plan, which I encountered when I served on a ULI advisory services panel there, represents a responsible effort to find viable middle ground on the development continuum somewhere between high-density and low-density sprawl. Many cities need to adopt Bloomington's balanced view on their zoning boards and planning commissions. These agencies should not be rubber stamps for either developers or conservationists, "growthers" or "no-growthers." I have heard environmentalists in Indianapolis complain that no thought is given to trees and green space and habitat protection and developers complain that the bureaucracy is micromanaging them. Bloomington steers a middle course, which is where the truth usually lies. The city understands compactness as the opposite of urban sprawl, that is, "low-density development; discontinuous and disorganized growth; and ribbon or strip development." In the name of a more compact urban form, the Bloomington plan encourages higher residential development densities to reduce land consumption, putting new development only where public infrastructure exists to serve it, and directing growth "where it is desirable, where it is in the public interest to grow, and where options conducive to future growth can be exercised."

Look also at Lowertown, an urban village in St. Paul, Minnesota, along the city's lower Mississippi River landing, funded by the McKnight Foundation and designed by Weiming Lu, an architect known as the Zen master of urban design and administration. It combines recycled historic buildings and artfully designed new ones with computer-based businesses linked globally through extensive fiber optics and satellite uplinks. Some call it a "cyber-village."[77] It certainly provides a useful example of sustainable development at its best. It has its own shared heating and air conditioning through underground conduits, reducing energy use and pollution. It offers offices, homes, jobs, urban parks, street art, and entertainment.

Another example of compact urban development comes from Orlando, Florida. Public policies that reward good development and discourage the bad are the key to promoting good sprawl, or quality growth—and in this city, that is exactly what's being done. Concerned about the traffic congestion, crime, and school problems that a 3.5 percent annual growth rate has brought, Orlando and Orange County put a growth barrier into place in response to Florida's state-mandated 1991 comprehensive plan. The purpose was to avoid more leapfrog development. Even with the barrier in place, the area's 1.4 million inhabitants are far from evenly concentrated. City government and owners of multiple tracts southeast of the city therefore are preparing a master plan and development standards for a 12,000-acre site. According to Reid Ewing:

The plan itself is neotraditional, featuring neighborhood, village, and town centers that are compact and walkable. It provides for jobs/housing balance—specifically, for 29,000 residential units and millions of square feet of retail, office and industrial space. It preserves more than 40 percent of the total land area as parks or natural open spaces in a clustered pattern.

Property owners have bought into the plan because it promises more dwelling units (at higher net densities) and more commercial space (at higher FARs—floor/area ratios) than would a standard suburban master plan. They have also come to realize that compact, mixed-use development, with quality features, will sell better than sprawl.[78]

New Urbanism

Initially dubbed neotraditional planning, "new urbanism" is an approach to compact community development and revitalization based on traditional neighborhood development patterns. An alternative to suburban sprawl, new urbanism seeks to reintegrate housing, workplace, shopping, and recreation into compact, pedestrian-friendly, mixed-use neighborhoods linked by transit. Proponents of the movement argue that these principles can lead to lower consumption of land, reduced reliance on automobiles, reduced service costs, and development that is more compatible with existing neighborhoods. On a social level, supporters of new urbanism see it as an antidote to the isolation and loss of the sense of community that some feel suburban sprawl has engendered.

The Congress for New Urbanism defines the basic principles of the movement as development in the form of compact, walkable neighborhoods with clearly defined centers and edges; grid-patterned, interconnected streets that encourage pedestrian activity without wholly excluding the automobile; and building entrances that front the street rather than a parking lot. All of the components of a functioning community should be laid out in proximity, and a wide spectrum of housing options should be available to enable residents of different ages, incomes, and family types to live within a single neighborhood or district. Civic buildings should be sited in prominent locations, and parks, playgrounds, and other open spaces should be conveniently located throughout a neighborhood.

The new urbanism movement draws its inspiration from early–20th century community designs, many of which remain successful today. An example is the Country Club District in Kansas City, Missouri. In 1908, developer J.C. Nichols and a group of investors gained control of 1,000 acres of land on Kansas City's south side, calling it the Country Club District to emphasize its proximity to the Kansas City Country Club. Nichols began to develop homes and invested heavily in community facilities, such as landscaped parks and public art. At the center of the community, Nichols built a retail and office complex called Country Club Plaza. The development eventually contained 6,000 houses, 160 apartment buildings, and 35,000 residents. Then, as now, this neighborhood was considered the "in" place to live and shop.

A recent development that employs the principles of new urbanism is Kentlands, in suburban Washington, D.C. The 352-acre planned community uses traditional neighborhood and community design to create a small-town feeling. The design relies on a hierarchy of streets built in a modified grid, with most homes close to the street on small lots ranging from 2,500 to 9,000 square feet. On-street parking is permitted throughout the project and, in most cases, garages are placed behind houses. The community incorporates a variety of housing types—including detached and attached homes, apartments, and condominiums—often on the same street. Shared open space is an important element that complements the small lots, and numerous small parks and squares are located throughout the neighborhood. Among Kentlands's amenities are a 350,000-square-foot shopping center, an elementary school, a children's center, and a church.

But the best-known example of neotraditionalism is probably the first new urbanist project, Seaside, in the Florida panhandle. Designed and planned by Andres Duany and Elizabeth Plater-Zyberk of Miami, along with consultants Robert A.M. Stern of New York and Leon Krier of London, Seaside is an 80-acre site that runs parallel to the Gulfside beach. The street pattern for this town (it's a lot more than just beach houses or a typical suburban subdivision) is drawn from small-town archetypes that favor walking over driving. Public buildings, civic spaces, townhouses, apartments, offices, and retail activity are organized around a town center defined by a geometric, hierarchical system of roads and pathways. Codes carefully spell out design standards for yards, porches, outbuildings, picket fences, setbacks, deep roof overhangs, parking, wood construction, and building heights. Amenities like tennis courts, beach pavilions, pools, and green space are scattered throughout Seaside. This architectural gem creates a community of beauty and joy, because its "residents can enjoy an unspoiled beach environment while experiencing small-town life focused around an old-fashioned town square."[79]

A successful city will seek to make living comfortable and compatible with the community fabric. By using street grids instead of culs-de-sac, narrow streets instead of wide ones, sidewalks at the curb, on-street parking, shallow setbacks, semienclosed spaces like village greens and plazas instead of wide-open spaces like greenbelts and golf courses, shopping on Main Street rather than in enclosed malls and strip centers, and mixed-use (not single-use) neighborhoods, the neotraditional vision of community—whether it is found in Loudoun County, Virginia, or Laguna West in Sacramento, California—offers something of value to potential buyers. It offers shorter or less-congested distances to travel, opportunities for leisure pursuits, good-quality and affordable housing, and a general improvement in lifestyle.[80]

California-based planner and writer William Fulton concludes, "the most refreshing aspect of this movement (new urbanism) is that it promotes a positive image of 'town life' that includes the public as well as the private realm. And in a world where a 'lack of community' is often blamed for many social ills, this is no small achievement."[81]

A lot of people in the land use business don't seem to like the idea of smart growth much. It conjures in their minds the hobgoblin of "big brother" looking over their shoulder, telling them what they can and cannot do. But I believe they misunderstand the concept. Smart growth is a strategic approach, a program, a set of goals, a process, NOT a set of bureaucratic regulations. It requires planning on a comprehensive, integrated, regional basis and usually involves both public and private sectors. Smart growth is not incompatible with development. It is, however, the opposite of mindless sprawl, for it enhances a community's vitality, economic well-being, and environmental quality, using tax dollars efficiently while attracting private investment.

If we are to succeed in the revitalization of our cities and towns, communities and their leaders should keep smart growth from becoming a political issue. St. Louis, to cite one example, is vexed by political criticism of efforts to plan for wiser regionwide growth. Accusations of one political party are hurled at the other, and suspicion has replaced trust, hampering efforts at renewal.

In sum, the goals of a smart-growth program are:

- Maintenance of a high quality of life and sense of community;
- Creation of user-friendly neighborhoods and urban entertainment districts;

- Decreasing dependence on the automobile, with a commitment to easy movement and security;
- Encouragement of infill construction, mixed-use development, and growth where infrastructure is already in place;
- Preservation of historic buildings;
- Promotion of adaptive use;
- Renewal of brownfields and abandoned lands;
- Protection of the environment and natural resources; and
- Provision of adequate services with identification of clear boundaries for future urban growth.

America's central cities can reverse the trend of decline that has characterized the last quarter of the 20th century and begin a cycle of renewal that makes them relevant and vital to the emerging economy of the 21st century. The key to their revitalization is to draw the middle class—black and white and brown—back downtown. National and regional economies cannot thrive and compete without successful cities. The optimistic views of urban planning consultant William H. Whyte are encouraging. In his book, *City: Rediscovering the Center,* Whyte recognizes that "the city has been losing those functions for which it is no longer competitive," such as back-office business, manufacturing, and what he calls "the computers." But Whyte concludes: "I think (the center) is going to hold . . . because of the way people demonstrate by their actions how vital is centrality. . . . [A]s the city has been losing functions it has been reasserting its most ancient one: [to be] a place where people come together, face-to-face."[82]

With strong leadership, the best days of our cities lie ahead, not behind.

CITYSHIP CREATES "PLACES WORTHY OF OUR AFFECTION." THAT IS THE FINAL PART OF MY VISION FOR CITIES THAT WILL CONTINUE TO REBOUND IN THE 21ST CENTURY.

EPILOGUE

WE END, AS WE BEGAN, with Philadelphia.

Mayor Ed Rendell and some of his close associates, who have been at the center of their city's comeback, share a conviction "that the recovery of American cities is more wishful than real, more skin-deep than systemic." Says Rendell: "This is not a happy thing for a mayor to say, but I think the fundamental problems of the city are being papered over and that we look a whole lot better than we really are." He sounds a tocsin: Beware of overestimating the reported comeback of cities. It's the old Gilbert and Sullivan message: "Things are seldom what they seem; skimmed milk masquerades as cream." The author of *A Prayer for the City,* Buzz Bissinger, in his analysis of Philadelphia's current condition, calls Rendell's city a "manufacturing mausoleum." He claims that downtown has become "a kind of stage set in every city, beyond which are acres and acres of despair." The successes of the mayors in other cities that he mentions (Baltimore, Detroit, Atlanta, Washington, Miami, Cleveland, and Newark) "are being undermined by an inexorable demographic rot." Depopulation and a fundamental mismatch between the limited job skills of people left in the inner city and the highly skilled, postindustrial jobs that cities now offer lie below the water line on the urban iceberg. It is easier for state and federal officials to focus on the successes. Such "starry-eyed assumptions are cheap, easy, and go down nicely with tax-averse suburbanites." So "the notion that American cities have somehow turned a corner becomes an excuse for slashing programs, such as welfare, that primarily benefit people who live in cities."[1]

But I cannot dwell in a cave of such despair. There has to be more to the story than the dirge: "Look on my works, O ye mighty, and despair." Philadelphia may be dying, as Rendell says, but it would be much deader without his outstanding leadership and that of many others. The city's structural problems are severe, and one could never say it is a sparkling city like Boston, Houston, Denver, Seattle, San Francisco, Orlando, or New York. Nonetheless, while it may be true that Philadelphia is a "manufacturing mausoleum," it also may be true that the city is in the midst of a transition from the 20th to the 21st century—that is, from an old city to a new one, from an industrial machine that supplied most of the jobs in the region, to a Third Wave, flattened-out, decentralized metropolis, with thriving edge cities, struggling inner-ring suburbs, and a downtown that has tourism, entertainment, and culture at its heart. Certainly the mood in Philadelphia is upbeat, from what I conclude after a number of interviews there.

So let's not throw in the towel for the cities. They endured a period of decline, with all the attendant problems: racial isolation, neighborhood deterioration, smog, congestion, old infrastructure, abandoned buildings, crime, and jobs moving to the suburbs. But hopeful signs do exist as urban America rounds the corner into the new millennium. Neighborhoods are rebuilding. New energy and vitality are appearing in downtowns. New housing, new business, and new investments are pursuing economic opportunities in the central city. Cities and suburbs are beginning to forge regional alliances. Grass-roots civic leadership is sprouting up all over the place, and different segments of communities are collaborating. Smart growth is curbing bad sprawl. Homeownership has risen to record levels. Cities are becoming less dependent on the federal government. Welfare programs are being reformed and public housing is less often warehousing tenants in high rises. Tenants are being encouraged to make the transition to ownership, and mixed-income, architecturally attractive, low-rise affordable homes and rentals are beginning to dot the urban streetscape. Cities are governing themselves better, more efficiently and effectively, and community policing seems to be having a salutary effect on crime rates. And the image Americans have of their cities has become more positive: cities are more often seen as centers of business, culture, and progress, rather than of poverty, crime, and other social problems.[2] Changes do not occur overnight, and the bullish economy of today may become a bear tomorrow. But forces seem to be converging from a number of different directions to

provide reasons for cautious optimism as new city structures proceed to replace old ones.

In August 1998, a gleaming hotel, the Hawthorne, opened in downtown Philadelphia. It is the first of ten or so new hotels (all with an eye on
the city's convention business) that will add 3,000 rooms to the center city.
Would investors be foolish enough to put their money into these projects if
they were going to be housed in a mausoleum? The Hawthorne's 294 rooms
occupy a glistening white frame building that used to be an old, dirty, 16-
story garment factory at 11th and Vine. A sign, perhaps? Anecdotal, to be
sure, like most of the examples in this book, not analytical. But does that in-
validate it? It depends on what lenses you look through. Philadelphia's pall-
bearers may be premature. A futurist observer of the Philadelphia scene,
Drexel University Professor Arthur B. Shostak, has written: "[We] can and
must shape a far more desirable urban future."[3] And was it not that most famous of all Philadelphians, Ben Franklin, who said: "We can make these times
better if we bestir ourselves?"

Take a drive or hike near sunset to Fairmount Park in Philadelphia or
for that matter, to Griffith Park (Los Angeles), the Brooklyn Heights prome-
nade (New York City), Mt. Washington (Pittsburgh), Federal Hill (Baltimore),
Camelback Mountain (Phoenix), Marin Headlands (San Francisco), Sandia
Peak (Albuquerque), Red Rocks (Denver), Ft. Smith (Washington, D.C.),
Queen Anne's Hill (Seattle)—or to any number of other high places that over-
look a city in this vast and wonderful country. See the sun set. Then watch
the city down below begin to twinkle with myriad points of light. The city is
alive, vital, pulsating, dynamic, not static, forever changing, eternally old,
eternally new, stumbling, rebounding, dying, and being reborn. Those who
love the cities of America and are dedicated to responsible land use and to
the art and practice of cityship may see a positive sign in these lights. They
are harbingers of hope, shining in the darkness, not being overcome by it.
Some have been extinguished, to be sure; they glow no longer. Others are
fluttering and faint, candles in the wind. But others are shimmering brightly
and beautifully, and new ones are being turned on even as you watch. And
then there are some lights that illuminate the night sky like beacons pointing

to the stars. Our calling is not to curse the darkness in the great metropolises and cities where we live. It is to keep the lights of urban America burning—not let them flicker out.

NOTES

CHAPTER 1

1. Matt Bai, "A Wing and a Prayer," *Newsweek,* January 15, 1998, 65.

2. David Osborne and Ted Gaebler, *Reinventing Government: How the Entrepreneurial Spirit is Transforming the Public Sector* (Reading, Mass.: Addison-Wesley Publishing, 1992), xix.

3. Peggy Dye, *Word from the George Bruce Library, Harlem* (New York City: Libraries for the Future, December 1995), 4.

4. Lewis Mumford, *The City in History* (New York: Harcourt, Brace, & World, Inc., 1961), 556.

5. Richard W. Judy and Carol D'Amico, *Workforce 2020: Work and Workers in the 21st Century* (Indianapolis: The Hudson Institute, 1997), 6-7.

6. *AIA Vision 2000: Shaping Architects' Future* (Washington, D.C.: AIA Press, May 1988) 12-13.

7. Alvin and Heidi Toffler, *Creating a New Civilization: The Politics of the Third Wave* (Atlanta: Turner Publishing, Inc., 1995), 106.

8. Richard Moe and Carter Wilkie, *Changing Places* (New York: Henry Holt, 1997), 40, 99.

CHAPTER 2

1. Alvin and Heidi Toffler, *Creating a New Civilization: The Politics of the Third Wave* (Atlanta: Turner Publishing Inc., 1995), 34.

2. Reid Ewing, "Is Los Angeles-Style Sprawl Desirable?," *Journal of the American Planning Association,* Winter 1997.

3. *Final Report of the Mayor's Task Force on Technology and the Future of the City* (Columbus, Ohio, May 8, 1998).

4. Louis Zacharilla, "Teleports: Hubs of Intelligent Cities," *The American City and County* (March 1998), 10ff.

5. Randy Arndt, "Cities Increase Service Levels, Range of Services," *Nation's Cities Weekly,* January 26, 1998, 1ff.

6. "Brighter Lights for Big Cities," *Business Week* (May 4, 1998), 88-95.

7. David Shenk, "No One Mingles in the Global Village," *USA Today* (June 17, 1997), 13A.

8. From a speech given by Paul Goldberger to the International Design Congress, May 1997, Jackson Hole, Wyoming.

9. Douglas Henton, John Melville, and Kimberly Walesh, *Grassroots Leaders for a New Economy: How Civic Entrepreneurs Are Building Prosperous Communities* (San Francisco: Jossey-Bass, Inc., 1997).

10. Neal Peirce, "The New Economy: Possible Friend, Not Foe, of America's Communities?" syndicated column (May 3, 1998).

11. Michael Beyard and Michael Rubin, "A New Industry Emerges," *Urban Land* supplement (August 1995), 6. See also Michael Beyard et al., *Developing Urban Entertainment Centers* (Washington, D.C.: Urban Land Institute, 1998).

12. "Pursuing Urban Entertainment: New York Conference Illuminates Power & Light Dis-

trict," *The Kansas City Business Journal* (March 6, 1998), 2; "Movies Make a Town Square," *Variety* (March 16, 1998), 1; "Tightlipped About Builders and Tenants," *The Kansas City Business Journal* (June 5, 1998), 3.

13. J. Robert Brown and Michele Laumer, "Comeback Cities," *Urban Land* (August 1995), 46-51, 83.

CHAPTER 3

1. Quoted in Neal Peirce and Curtis Johnson, *Boundary Crossers* (College Park, Md.: The Academy of Leadership Press, 1997), 9.

2. Speech to National Press Club, Washington, D.C., February 5, 1995.

3. The quotation from Vince Foster's suicide note appears in Robert H. Williams, "My Truth, Their Consequences," *Washington Post,* August 15, 1993, C05.

4. Charles Mahtesian, "The Politics of Ugliness," *Governing,* 1997, as reprinted in *Actionlines* by the Indiana Association of Cities and Towns, August 1997, 6ff.

5. These examples are taken from Peirce and Johnson, *Boundary Crossers.*

6. Peirce and Johnson, *Boundary Crossers,* table of contents (Lessons 5 and 7), 28, 34.

7. Richard W. Judy and Carol D'Amico, *Workforce 2020: Work and Workers in the 21st Century* (Indianapolis: The Hudson Institute, 1997), 5, 6, 53, 110.

8. Cornel West, *Race Matters* (New York: Vintage Books, 1994), 156.

9. *Vital Speeches,* June 15, 1993, 535.

10. West, *Race Matters,* 70.

11. Founded by Dwight D. Eisenhower in 1950 "to illuminate issues of public policy," the American Assembly is an affiliate of Columbia University that prepares consensus statements and recommendations addressed to policy makers. See the Ninety-First American Assembly, *Community Capitalism: Rediscovering the Markets of America's Urban Neighborhoods* (New York: Columbia University, 1997), 3, 4.

12. Ibid., 12-13.

13. Quoted in William H. Hudnut III, "The Entrepreneurial American City," *Princeton Alumni Weekly* (Princeton, N.J.: Princeton University), March 12, 1986, 21.

14. The material and quotes in this paragraph are from Mark Rosentraub, *Major League Losers* (New York: Harper-Collins, 1997), 294-296.

15. E.J. Dionne, Jr., "Cities, Governments and Individuals," *Washington Post,* Dec.12, 1997, A 29.

16. Neal Peirce, "Building a City of Choices," syndicated column, February 15, 1998.

17. Neal Peirce, "Bring on the Civic Entrepreneurs," syndicated column, May 11, 1997.

18. Ibid.

19. Toffler, *Creating a New Civilization,* 98.

20. Douglas Henton, John Melville, and Kimberly Walesh, *Grassroots Leaders for a New Economy: How Civil Entrepreneurs Are Building Prosperous Communities* (San Francisco: Jossey-Bass, Inc., 1997), 47, 77.

21. John W. Gardner, foreword to Peirce and Johnson, *Boundary Crossers,* ii, iii.

CHAPTER 4

1. Fred Hiatt, "How Good Will Come From Globalization," *Washington Post,* June 16, 1997, A 21.

2. Peter Schwartz and Peter Lyden, "The Long Boom: A History of the Future, 1980-2020," *Wired,* July 1997, 2.

3. *Global Dollars, Local Sense: Cities and Towns in the International Economy* (Washington, D.C.: National League of Cities, 1993), 2.

4. Peter Drucker, "The Age of Social Transformation," *The Atlantic Monthly,* November 1994, 66, 68.

5. John Naisbitt, *Global Paradox* (New York: Avon Books, 1995).

6. Jeremy Main, "How to Go Global—and Why," *Fortune,* August 28, 1989, 70.

7. James Brooks, *Leading Cities in a Global Economy* (Washington, D.C.: National League of Cities, 1995), iii.

8. Ibid., 95-99.

9. Brooks, *Leading Cities in a Global Economy.*

10. "Renewing Cities," unpublished in 1998 business plan (New Orleans: Historic Restoration Inc.), 1.

11. For a more complete listing of case studies, see Joe DiStefano and Matthew Raimi, *Five Years of Progress: 110 Communities Where ISTEA Is Making a Difference* (Washington, D.C.: Surface Transportation Policy Project, 1997).

12. James Fishkin, "No Way to Run a Town Meeting," *Washington Post,* February 27, 1998, A 25.

13. For a more complete discussion of RCOs, see William R. Dodge, *Regional Ex-cellence* (Washington, D.C.: National League of Cities, 1996), 270ff.

14. Peirce and Johnson, "The Peirce Report on Indianapolis," *The Indianapolis Star and News,* November 10-17, 1996, 5.

15. Kevin McCarty, "City/County Metro Economies Drive National Economic Boom," *U.S. Mayor,* March 26, 1998, 1.

16. Robert Stein, Richard Murray, and Gregory Weiher, *Greater Houston: The Regional Dilemma* (Houston: Center for Houston's Future, The Greater Houston Partnership, 1996), 30.

17. Ibid., 4-19.

18. Stein, Murray, and Weiner, *Greater Houston.*

19. Allan Wallis, "Town Meeting: Regional Governance," white paper, Town Meeting West, Denver, 12-13.

20. Ibid.

21. Dodge, *Regional Excellence,* 250.

22. Dodge, 287.

23. Dodge, 288.

24. Dodge, 280.

25. John Buechner, *Regional Governance in the Denver Metropolitan Area,* Report to Denver Metro Forum, December 1991, 13.

26. Neal Peirce and Curtis Johnson, *Boundary Crossers* (College Park, Md.: The Academy of Leadership Press, 1997), 8.

27. *Emerging Trends in Real Estate 1998* (New York: ERE Yarmouth and Real Estate Research Corporation, October 1997), on-line report.

28. Quoted in *The Better Community Catalog: A Sourcebook for Ideas, People, and*

Strategies for Improving the Place Where You Live (Washington, D.C.: Acropolis Books, 1989), 180.

29. Ibid., 181.

30. Jo Allen Gause, *New Uses for Obsolete Buildings* (Washington, D.C.: Urban Land Institute, 1996), 25.

31. Neal Peirce, Renee Berger, Farley Peters, and Carol Steinbach, *Market Standards, Community Dividend: Economically Targeted Investments for the '90s* (Washington, D.C.: A Report to the National Academy of Public Administration, February 1994), 35.

32. Mike Miles, Richard L. Haney, and Gayle L. Berens, *Real Estate Development: Principles and Process,* second edition (Washington, D.C.: Urban Land Institute, 1996), 167.

33. Neal Peirce and Curtis Johnson, "The Peirce Report on St. Louis," *St. Louis Post-Dispatch,* March 16, 1997, 10.

34. Ibid.

35. Carl V. Patton, "The Value of a University in an Urban Setting," remarks delivered at the University of Cincinnati, March 3, 1995.

36. Peirce and Johnson, "The Peirce Report on St. Louis," 13.

CHAPTER 5

1. David Osborne and Peter Plastrik, *Banishing Bureaucracy: The Five Strategies for Reinventing Government* (Reading, Mass.: Addison-Wesley Publishing, 1997), 9.

2. Peter Drucker, *Innovation and Entrepreneurship* (New York: Harper & Row, 1986), 186-187.

3. Stephen Goldsmith, *The Twenty-First Century City: Resurrecting Urban America* (Washington, D.C.: Regnery Publishing, 1997), 9.

4. Frank Shafroth, "President Schwartz Rallies Local Officials behind Five-Pronged Agenda," *Nation's Cities Weekly,* March 17, 1997, 4.

5. For a complete analysis, see Neal Peirce, "'Kobans' and 'Safe Havens'—The Formula We've Been Waiting For?" syndicated column, February 22, 1998.

6. Timothy D. Crowe and Diane L. Zahm, "Crime Prevention Through Environmental Design," *Land Development* (Fall 1994), 22.

7. Oscar Newman, *Defensible Space: Crime Prevention Through Urban Design* (New York: The MacMillan Company, 1972), 3.

8. See David Parham, "Crime Prevention Through Real Estate Development and Management," ULI Education Policy Forum Series #650, 1995.

9. Ibid.

10. Thomas Vonier, "Urban Security Zones," *Urban Land* (January 1997), 6-7.

11. Frederick Heller, "Circling The Wagons: The Controversy over Gated Communities," *Real Estate Outlook* (November 1995), 7.

12. See "Dropout Rates in the United States, 1996," The National Center for Education Statistics.

13. Goldsmith, *The Twenty-First Century City,* 121.

14. Bruno Manno and Gregg Vanourek, "White House Disables Charter School Movement," *Foresight,* vol. 1, no. 12 (Indianapolis: Hudson Institute, December 1997), 1, 4.

15. In Indiana, the welfare benefits package reaches $7.50 an hour, according to an Indiana University professor; it reaches $9.20 as estimated by the Cato Institute. See Goldsmith, *Twenty-First Century City,* 98.

16. Ibid. 105-106.

17. Goldsmith, *Twenty-First Century City,* 113.

18. Special advertising feature, *Newsweek,* May 19, 1997.

19. Goldsmith, *Twenty-First Century City,* 112, 123.

20. *Changing Construction Markets: The Next Fifteen Years* (Washington, D.C.: The American Institute of Architects, 1996), 10.

21. *Leadership for Learning* (Arlington, Va.: American Association of School Administrators, undated).

22. See Margaret Garb, "TriBeCa: From Quiet, Desolate Streets To High-Priced Neighborhood," *New York Times,* November 2, 1997, and Frank McGurty, "Paying for Prestige and a Room with a View," *The Financial Times,* May 28, 1994.

23. Cited in White House briefing papers accompanying introduction of The Partnership to Rebuild America's Schools Act, March 14, 1997.

24. David Vise and Debbi Wilgoren, "D.C. Repairs of Schools Criticized," *Washington Post,* January 13, 1998, 1.

25. Speech by Maryland governor Parris Glendening to the Partners for Smart Growth Conference co-sponsored by Urban Land Institute and USEPA in Baltimore, Maryland, December 3, 1997.

26. Changing Construction Markets, 7.

27. *America's Real Estate* (Washington, D.C.: Urban Land Institute, 1997), 32.

28. Stuart Steers, "Suddenly, Center-City Housing Is Hot," *Denver Business Journal,* August 12, 1994, 13B(2).

29. John R. Pitkin et al., *Immigration and Housing in the United States: Trends and Prospects,* Immigration Research Project (Washington, D.C.: Fannie Mae Foundation, 1997).

30. Joseph Schwartz, "Coming to America," *Forecast* (March/April 1996), 22.

31. *A Brief Look at Postwar U.S. Income Inequality* (U.S. Bureau of Census, June 1996), 60-191.

32. Reynolds Farley, Elaine Fielding, and Maria Krysan, "The Residential Preferences of Blacks and Whites: A Four-Metropolis Analysis," *Housing Policy Debate,* vol. 8, issue 4 (Washington, D.C.: Fannie Mae Foundation, 1997), 763 ff.

33. Neal Peirce, "Subsidized Housing: So Terrible After All?," syndicated column (April 13, 1997).

34. Charles Field, "Building Consensus for Affordable Housing," *Housing Policy Debate,* vol. 8, issue 4 (Washington,D.C.: Fannie Mae Foundation, 1997), 801 ff.

35. William Hudnut, *The Hudnut Years in Indianapolis* (Bloomington: Indiana University Press, 1995), 37.

36. Robert L. Woodson, Sr., *The Triumphs of Joseph* (New York: The Free Press, 1998), 48.

37. Ibid., 46.

38. Diane Suchman, with Margaret Sowell, *Developing Infill Housing in Inner-City Neighborhoods: Opportunities and Strategies* (Washington, D.C.: Urban Land Institute, 1997), 1.

39. Ibid., foreword by Lloyd Bookout, vi.

40. Suchman, *Infill Housing,* 33.

41. Philip Langdon, "Housing for a Town Center," *Builder Online* (July 1998).

42. Suchman, *Infill Housing,* 77-81.

43. Charles E. Fraser, unpublished manuscript for a book on greenbelt towns.

44. Vernon Swaback, *Designing the Future* (Tempe: Arizona State University, 1998), 49.

45. *USA Today,* December 27, 1996.

46. Jo Allen Gause, *New Uses for Obsolete Buildings* (Washington, D.C.: Urban Land Institute,1996), 121-126.

47. Ibid., 17.

48. *Kenosha's Harborpark Master Plan* (Kenosha, Wis.: September 1997), 2-4.

49. U.S. Department of Transportation, *1997 Status of the Nation's Surface Transportation System—Condition and Performance.*

50. Mary Boehling Schwartz, "Airports: Prospects for Future Development," working paper 644 (Washington, D.C.: Urban Land Institute, 1993), 81.

51. Robert Dunphy, *Transportation and Growth, Myth and Fact* (Washington, D.C.: Urban Land Institute, 1996), 6.

52. *Evening Minute* (Washington, D.C.: The Greater Washington Board of Trade, July 15, 1997).

53. Transit Cooperative Research Program, *Building Transit Ridership: An Exploration of Transit's Market Share and the Public Policies That Influence It* (Washington, D.C.: National Academy Press, 1997), 2.

54. M. Replogle, "Bicycle Access to Public Transportation: Learning from Abroad," *ITE Journal* (December 1992), 15.

55. Anthony Downs, *New Visions for Metropolitan America* (Washington, D.C. and Cambridge, Mass.: The Brookings Institution and The Lincoln Institute of Land Policy, 1994), 154.

56. Ibid., 155.

57. Aileen Cho, "Linking at Last," *Engineering News Record* (March 9, 1998), 36-38.

58. *U.S. Mayor,* vol. 65, issue 5 (March 26, 1998), 1 ff. and *U.S. Mayor,* vol. 65, issue 10 (June 1, 1998), 1 ff.

59. For rapid bus transit plan, see http://www.ci.eugene.or.us.

60. Edward A. Lenny, *Indianapolis: The Story of a City* (Indianapolis and New York: Bobbs Merrill, 1971), 87, 173.

61. "Sunset Roads for the Future," *Washington Post,* July 28, 1997, A18.

62. Richard Moe and Carter Wilkie, *Changing Places: Rebuilding Community in the Age of Sprawl* (New York: Henry Holt, 1998), 83.

63. William Hudnut, "Saving Cities," *The San Diego Union-Tribune,* December 5, 1993, G1, 6.

64. "Transit Villages for BART stations," *San Mateo County Times,* August 4, 1998.

65. Philip Langdon, "Transit-Friendly Housing," *Builder Online,* July 1998.

66. C.J. Canino, "Transit-Based Housing to Be a Model," *San Jose Mercury News,* March 5, 1998.

67. John D. Kasarda, "An Industrial/Aviation Complex for the Future," *Urban Land,* August 1991, 16ff.

68. John D. Kasarda, "The Global Transpark," *Urban Land,* April 1998, 107ff.

69. Clinton V. Oster, Jr., et al., "Economic Impacts of Transportation Investments: The Case of Federal Express," *Transportation Journal* (Winter 1997), 34-44.

70. *America's Real Estate* (Washington, D.C.: Urban Land Institute, 1997), 18.

71. Ibid., 19.

72. "New Institute to Study the Nation's Infrastructure Ills," *Engineering News Record,* February 2, 1998, 7.

73. Goldsmith, *Twenty-First Century City,* 86.

74. Gregg Easterbrook, "Here Comes the Sun," *The New Yorker,* April 10, 1995.

75. Susan Maxman & Partners, firm overview materials.

76. Ibid.

77. Clifford Pearson, "Developer Brings Green Ideas to the Spec Market," *Architectural Record,* June 1997, 73.

78. Ibid., 75.

79. Pearson, "Green Ideas," 73.

80. James Howard Kunstler, "Home from Nowhere," *The Atlantic Monthly,* September 1996, 43ff.

81. Keith Schneider, "Suburban Sprawl," *Nieman Reports* (Cambridge, Mass.: Harvard University Press, Winter 1996).

82. *Final Report of the National Wildlife Conservation/Economic Development Dialogue* (Chevy Chase, Md.: Growth Management Institute/Environment Law Institute, March 1996).

83. Ibid.

84. David Rusk, *Cities Without Suburbs* (Washington, D.C.: Woodrow Wilson Press, 1993), 20.

85. *APA Growing Smart Newsletter,* Summer 1997.

86. *Recycling America's Land: A National Report on Brownfields Redevelopment* (Washington, D.C.: The United States Conference of Mayors, January 1998).

87. Neal Peirce, "Mayors Bask in Sudden Popularity," syndicated column, February 8, 1998.

CHAPTER 6

1. Thanks to James Howard Kunstler for the phrase "places worthy of our affection," which appeared in "Home from Nowhere," *The Atlantic Monthly,* vol. 278, no. 3, September 1996, 43ff.

2. Michael Ybarra, "Putting City Sprawl on a Zoning Diet," *New York Times,* June 16, 1996, E4.

3. Governor Parris Glendening, "Getting Smart About Sprawl," *Washington Post,* March 30, 1997, C08.

4. Robert W. Burchell, "Understanding Sprawl," *On the Ground* (Conference Proceedings of the Michigan State University Land-Use Forum), vol. 2, no. 2 (Lansing: Michigan State University, 1996), 13.

5. Ibid.

6. Neal Peirce, "Farmland Loss: Squandering a Birthright," syndicated column , March 23, 1997.

7. Ibid.

8. Maryanna Towler, "Urban Journal," (Rochester New York) *City Newspaper,* July 16-22, 1997.

9. Tischler & Associates, *Fiscal & Economic Newsletter,* no. 33, 1-2.

10. Reid Ewing, "Is Los Angeles–Style Sprawl Desirable?" *Journal of the American Planning Association* (Winter 1997), 6.

11. Mike and Peggy Dobbins, "Sprawl Things Considered: Controlling Growth," *American City & County* (September 1997), 28.

12. Robert Fishman, as quoted by Karl Zinmeister, "Are Today's Suburbs Really Family-Friendly?" *The American Enterprise,* November/December 1996, 39.

13. Roberta Maynard, "The Ripple Effect," *Builder Online,* July 1998.

14. Douglas Porter and Lindell Marsh, "When the Gnatcatcher Meets the Bulldozer," *Urban Land* (April 1994), 65ff.

15. Ewing, "Sprawl Things," 11.

16. James Howard Kunstler, "Zoning Procedures and Suburban Sprawl: A Cartoon of Human Habitat," *Vital Speeches* (December 15, 1997), 144.

17. "America's Cities," *The Economist,* January 10, 1998, 17-19.

18. Dennis R. Judd, *The Politics of American Cities,* 3d ed. (New York: Harper Collins, 1988), 155.

19. Kevin Heubusch, "Small Is Beautiful," *American Demographics* (January 1998), 43-49.

20. Judd, *The Politics of American Cities,* 192.

21. Theodore Hershberg, "The Case for Regional Cooperation," *The Regionalist* (Fall 1995) 13–22.

22. Peter Dreier, "Making the Case for Cities," *Challenge,* July-August 1995.

23. John D. Kasarda, Stephen J. Appold, Stuart H. Sweeney, and Elaine Sieff, "Central City and Suburban Migration Patterns: Is a Turnaround on the Horizon?" *Housing Policy Debate,* vol. 8, no. 2 (Washington, D.C.: Fannie Mae Foundation, 1997), 307ff.

24. Ibid, 325, 343.

25. *1998 Investment Strategy Annual* (Chicago: LaSalle Advisors Capital Management, Inc., 1998), 35.

26. Telephone conversation with Pittsburgh AP reporter, March 24, 1998.

27. Judith Havemann, "'Civic Entrepreneurs Boost Declining Cities," *Washington Post,* December 9, 1997, A1.

28. Quoted from the *Kansas City Star* by the Brookings Institution's Center on Urban and Metropolitan Policy, memorandum, Dae Nguyen, August 10, 1998.

29. According to Tracy Cross, a consultant to the homebuilding industry, June 5, 1998.

30. *Housing Policy Debate,* vol. 8, no. 2, 1997, 300.

31. Melissa Herron, "Brave New World," *Builder Online,* July 1998.

32. Bill Vlasic, "Motown in Motion," *Business Week,* April 21, 1997, 136ff.

33. *Detroit News,* April 13, 1997, quoted in *Architectural Record,* "Press Roundup," June 1997, 39.

34. Bill Vlasic, "Motown in Motion," *Business Week,* April 21, 1997, 136ff.

35. Bob Herbert, "The Missing Headline," *New York Times,* August 3, 1997, E13.

36. G. Thomas Kingsley et al., *Community Building: Coming of Age* (Baltimore: Development Training Institute, 1997), 9.

37. "American Cities: They Can Be Resurrected," *The Economist,* January 10, 1998, 18.

38. Neal Peirce "The Peirce Report," *St. Louis-Post Dispatch,* March 16, 1997.

39. See Neal Peirce et al., "Market Standards, Community Dividends: ETIs for the '90s," *A Report to the National Academy of Public Administration,* February 1994, 29.

40. Rob Gurwitt, "Saving the Aging Suburb," *Governing Magazine,* May 1993, 38.

41. Anthony Downs, "Suburban/Inner-City Ecosystem," *Journal of Property Management,* November-December 1997, 60ff.

42. Susan Garland and Peter Galuszka, "The 'Burbs Fight Back," *Business Week,* June 2, 1997, 147.

43. Jane Braxton Little, "Cities' Decaying First-Ring Suburbs Unite to Survive," originated from American News Service, Knight-Ridder/Tribune News Service, March 11,1998, 11, as reprinted by the Information Access Company.

44. Gurwitt, "Saving the Aging Suburb," 42.

45. Herbert Muschamp, "Becoming Unstuck on the Suburbs," *New York Times,* October 19,1997.

46. William Hudnut, *The Hudnut Years in Indianapolis* (Bloomington: Indiana University Press, 1995), 32.

47. For a complete discussion of this topic, see Jo Allen Gause, *New Uses for Obsolete Buildings* (Washington, D.C.: Urban Land Institute, 1996). This quotation and the ones that follow in this section are taken from that book.

48. David Rusk, *Cities Without Suburbs* (Washington, D.C.: The Woodrow Wilson Center Press, 1993), 22.

49. Lawrence O. Houstoun, Jr., *BIDs: Business Improvement Districts* (Washington, D.C.: Urban Land Institute, in cooperation with the International Downtown Association, 1997), 8.

50. Richard Moe and Carter Wilkie, *Changing Places* (New York: Henry Holt & Co., 1997), 85-87.

51. Robert D. Russell, Jr., and Eugene J. Johnson, *Memphis: An Architectural Guide* (Knoxville, Tenn.: University of Tennessee Press, 1990), 62, quoted by Moe and Wilkie, 86.

52. Moe and Wilkie, *Changing Places,* 90-91, 94.

53. Ibid., 91.

54. Transcript, *The Knoxville Mayors' Forum* (Washington, D.C.: Urban Land Institute, 1997), 25.

55. Vernon Swaback, *Designing the Future* (Tempe: Arizona State University, 1998), 105.

56. Hudnut, *The Hudnut Years in Indianapolis*, 83.

57. Stephen Moore and Dean Stansel, *The Myth of America's Underfunded Cities* (Washington, D.C.: Cato Institute Policy Analysis #188, February 22,1993), 4.

58. Harold Wolman et al., "National Urban Economic Development Policy," *Journal of Urban Affairs*, vol. 14, nos. 3/4, 1992), 226, 229.

59. John Kain and Joseph Persky, *Alternatives to the Gilded Ghetto*, as quoted in Anthony Downs, *New Visions for Metropolitan America* (Washington, D.C.: The Brookings Institution, 1994), 101-102.

60. William H. Hudnut III, "Saving Cities: Enterprise Zones Could Help Revive Decaying Urban Neighborhoods," *San Diego Union-Tribune*, December 5, 1993, G 1, 6; Hudnut, "Gold at the End of the Urban Rainbow," *Indianapolis Star*, June 22, 1994, A-11; and Anthony Downs, *New Visions for Metropolitan America* (Washington, D.C.: The Brookings Institution, 1994), 101-103, 242.

61. J. Thomas Black, "Extending the Debate on Sprawl," *Urban Land*, September 1996, 8.

62. James W. Wentling and Lloyd Bookout, *Density by Design* (Washington, D.C.: Urban Land Institute, 1992), iv.

63. Tom Walsh, "A Modest Proposal: Freeze the Urban Growth Boundary," *Earthword*, no. 4, 28-29.

64. Swaback, *Designing the Future*, 33.

65. Zane Yost, "Riverplace," in Wentling and Bookout, *Density by Design*, 102-107.

66. California Center for Land Recycling letter, April 1, 1998, and CCLR Policy Paper #1.

67. *Growing Sensibly: A Guidebook of Best Development Practices in the Chicago Region* (Chicago: Metropolitan Planning Council, January 1998), 1-12.

68. Parris Glendening, speech, ULI/USEPA Conference on Smart Growth, Dec. 3, 1997, Baltimore.

69. Rick Cole, Nancy Gragaro, and Judy Corbett, "New Strategies for Promoting Urban Infill," *Urban Land*, September 1996, 37.

70. Quoted in Joel Garreau, *Edge City: Life on the New Frontier* (New York: Anchor Books/Doubleday, 1991), 47.

71. Jane Jacobs, *The Death and Life of Great American Cities* (New York: Random House, 1961), 429ff.

72. David Clayton, "Las Vegas Goes for Broke: Growth Is Good, Say Local Officials—Despite Water Shortages and Overcrowded Schools," *Planning*, vol. 61, no. 9 (September 1995), 4-6.

73. Speech by Governor Christine Todd Whitman, Raritan Valley Country Club, Bridgewater, N.J., January 22, 1998.

74. Bruce W. McClendon, "Thunder in Paradise over Growth Management," *Urban Land*, October 1994, 47ff; Douglas R. Porter, "Facing Growth with a Plan," *Urban Land*, June 1992, 18ff.; Stuart Meck, "Rhode Island Gets It Right: The Little State With a Big Planning Program," *Planning*, November 1997, 10.

75. California Planning & Development Report, vol. 10, no. 6 (June 1995), 1.

76. Arthur C. Nelson, "Improving Urban Growth Boundary Design and Management," *Real Estate Finance* (Winter 1992), 11 ff; Douglas Porter, "Reassessing Urban Growth Boundaries," *Urban Land,* August 1991, 25-26.

77. Neal Peirce, "Cyber-villages: New City Recovery Formula," syndicated column, March 9, 1997.

78. Reid Ewing, "Is Los Angeles-Style Sprawl Desirable?" *Journal of the American Planning Association,* 1997.

79. See Dean Schwanke et al., *Resort Development Handbook* (Washington, D.C.: Urban Land Institute, 1997), 334-337.

80. See Lloyd Bookout, "Neotraditional Town Planning: A New Vision for the Suburbs?" *Urban Land,* January 1992, 20-26.

81. William Fulton, "The New Urbanism Challenges Conventional Planning," *Landlines* (Cambridge, Mass.: Lincoln Institute of Land Policy, September 1996).

82. William H. Whyte, *City: Rediscovering the Center* (New York: Doubleday, 1988), 7, 341.

EPILOGUE

1. As quoted in Blaine Harden, "Rejuvenation of Cities: Was It Just Cosmetics?" *Washington Post,* March 15, 1998, A 3.

2. See *Fannie Mae National Housing Survey 1997* (Washington, D.C.: Fannie Mae, 1997), 5.

3. Arthur B. Shostak, "Scenarios of Change in Urban Environments," *Futures Research Quarterly,* Spring 1995, 18.

INDEX OF SELECTED NAMES AND PLACES

Abilene, TX, 37

Ada County Planning Association, 44

Albany, NY, 44

Albuquerque, NM, 128, 157

Alexandria, VA, 138

Allegheny County, PA, 40

America Works, 66-7

American Farmland Trust, 109

Ames, IA, 114

Anchorage, AL, 37

Antaramian, Mayor John, 84

Archer, Mayor Dennis, 34, 118

Ashe, Mayor Victor, 4, 133

Atlanta, 2, 23, 40, 74, 85, 117, 143-144, 155

Austin, TX, 32

Baltimore, 10, 18, 55, 114, 141-142, 155, 157

Bashkiroff, Nick, 18

Beck, Nuala, 6

Belz, Jack, 131-132

Bethesda, MD, 110, 143

Black, Tom, 137

Bloomington, IN, 148

Boise, ID, 44

Boston, 40, 43, 72, 78, 138, 156

Boulder, CO, 15, 75

Bradley, Senator Bill, 21-23

Bronx, 119

Brown, Mayor Willie, 64

Bryant Park (New York), 129-130

Buffalo, NY, 56

Burchell, Robert W., 109

California, 90, 110-112, 136, 152

California Public Employees Retirement
  System (CALPERS), 122

Campbell, Mayor Bill, 88

Canizaro, Joe, 4-5

Cato Institute, 134

Cedar Rapids, IA, 22-23, 117

Charleston, SC, 4, 133

Charlotte, NC, 23, 38

Chattanooga, TN, 24, 85

Chesapeake Bay, 105

Chicago, 40, 53, 54, 56-57, 75, 83-84, 88-89,
  99, 102-3, 109, 117-118, 123, 128, 138-139,
  143-144

Cincinnati, 99

Citizens League of Greater Cleveland, 45, 47

Clancey, Mayor Lee, 22-3

Clark County, OR, 32

Cleveland, 23, 47, 56, 81, 99, 113, 114, 117,
  119, 124, 155

Cleveland Heights, OH, 124

Coles, Mayor Brent, 4

Colorado Springs, CO, 38

Columbus, Ohio, 14, 37

Congress for New Urbanism, 150

Coors Field (Denver), 49

Corcoran, Mullins, Jennison, Inc., 78

Country Club District (Kansas City, MO), 150

Crystal City, VA, 143

Culver City, CA, 125

Cuomo, Secretary Andrew, 76

Daley, Mayor Richard, 4, 65, 70, 103

Dallas, 27, 38, 84, 88

Dayton, OH, 49

Decatur/Huntsville, AL, 40

Denver, 40, 49-50, 73, 83, 117, 156, 157

DePaul University, 57, 143

Design Center for American Urban
  Landscape, 125

Detroit, 19, 56, 89, 113-114, 117-119,
  121, 131, 155

Downs, Anthony, 87

Drucker, Peter, 36, 60

Duany, Andres, 151

Dunphy, Robert, 86, 88

Durst, Douglas, 97

Durst, Jonathan, 97

Dye, Peggy, 4

Eason, James, 45

East Orange, NJ, 37

Easterbrook, Gregg, 95-96

Endangered Species Act, 101

Enterprise Foundation, 55-56

Environmental Law Institute, 102

Environmental Protection Agency, 105

Euclid, OH, 124
Eugene, OR, 89
Evansville, IN, 136
Ewing, Reid, 13, 110, 112, 149
Fairfax, VA, 45
Feiner, Ed, 133, 141
Field, Charles, 76-7
Field of St. Croix (MN), 145
First Tier Consortium, 124
Fishman, Mary, 84
Florida, 59, 101, 117, 147, 149, 151
Fraser, Charles E., 81-82
Ft Lauderdale, 63, 71, 117
Ft. Worth, 83
Fullerton, CA, 112
Fulton, William, 152
Futrell, J. William, 102
Gardner, John W., 33
Giuliani, Mayor Rudy, 62
Glendening, Governor Parris, 72, 102, 141, 142, 147
Goldberger, Paul, 16
Goldsmith, Mayor Stephen, 61, 67
Graham, Mayor Nancy, 4
Grand Central Terminal (New York City), 30
Grand Valley Metro Council (MI), 41
Gray, Kimi, 77
Greater Houston Partnership, 46
Gretzky, Wayne, 9
Gund Arena, 47
Hampton, VA, 45
Harbor Point (Boston), 78
Harris, William H., 26
Harrisburg, PA, 129
Hartford, CT, 76, 114
Hawaii, 147
Hayes Valley (San Francisco), 64
Helmke, Mayor Paul, 103
Hempstead, 123
Henton, Douglas, 16
Herron, Joan, 40
Hershberg, Theodore, 115
Hilton Head, SC, 81
Hines Interests Limited Partnership, 121
Homan Square (Chicago), 80
Housing and Urban Development, U.S. Dept. of, 76, 78, 103, 127, 135

Houston, 40, 46, 48, 49, 112, 156
Hudson Institute, 24, 66
Huntsville, AL, 40
Indianapolis, 3, 9 10, 15, 18, 28-30, 40, 43, 46, 49, 50, 51, 56, 59, 60, 67, 72, 77, 78, 79, 81, 89, 95, 99, 100, 104, 109, 122, 126, 127, 133, 135
Intermodel Surface Transportation Efficiency Act (ISTEA), 44, 88
Ithaca, NY, 114
Jefferson County, KY, 49
Johnson, Curtis, 24, 39, 46, 51
Kabacoff, Pres, 39, 116
Kalamazoo, MI, 38
Kansas City, MO, 18, 56, 117, 145, 146, 150
Kasarda, John, 92-93
Kemmis, Dan, 44
Kemp, Jack, 135
Kenilworth-Parkside (Washington, DC), 77-78
Kenosha, WI, 84-85, 103
Kent County, MI, 41
Kentlands, MD, 151
Kentucky, 49
Kirk, Mayor Ron, 84
Knight, Mayor Bob, 41
Knoxville, TN, 133
Kunstler, James Howard, 98, 107, 113
Laguna West, CA, 152
Lake Elmo, MN, 145
Lakewood, OH, 124
Lamar Terrace Tax Increment Reinvestment Zone, Houston, TX, 49
Las Colinas, TX, 89
Las Vegas, 145
Lashutka, Mayor Greg, 14, 37
Latimer, George, 133
Lewandowski, Roberta, 80
Lieberman, Senator Joseph, 137
LionsGate (Redmond, WA), 80
Little Rock, AR 110
Local Initiatives Support Corporation (LISC), 55, 56
Los Angeles, 2, 14, 40, 70, 74, 80, 88, 89, 111, 113, 122, 125, 157
Loudoun County, VA, 45, 152
Louisville, KY, 49, 129
Lower Garden District (New Orleans), 4
Lowertown, MN, 149

Lu, Weiming, 149

Macon, GA, 117

Mandan-Bismarck-Burleigh-Morton (ND) Joint Service Network, 49

Marion County, IN, 43, 46

Maryland, 49, 107, 141, 142

Maxman, Susan, 97

Mays, Bill, 26

McCaleb, Mayor Gary, 37

McColl, Hugh, 23

McCormack Baron & Associates, 74, 146

MCI Center (Washington, DC), 17

McLean, Dan, 118

Memphis, 99, 104, 131, 132

Mentor, OH, 7

Miami, FL, 99, 151, 155

Middletown, DE, 111

Minneapolis, 124

Minnesota, 43, 124

Missoula, MT, 44

Mobile, AL, 117

Morgan, Linda, 90-91

Morgantown, WV, 114

Morrish, William, 125

Mount Vernon, VA, 114

Mt. Pleasant Homes (Cleveland), 81

Mumford, Lewis, 5, 11, 116

Murphy, Mayor Thomas, 117

Nashville/Davidson County, TN, 50

National Association of Home Builders, 76, 112

National Association of Regional Councils, 39

National League of Cities, 15, 36, 62

Natural Communities Conservation Program, 112

Neighborhood Reinvestment Corporation, 55

Nelson, Priscilla, 94

New Community Corporation, 55

New Haven, CT, 139

New Jersey, 42, 110, 111, 124, 144, 146, 147

New Orleans, 4, 5, 39, 43, 116, 129

New York, 4, 37, 40, 43, 71, 74, 75, 97, 110, 113, 129, 130, 135, 138, 151, 157

Newark, NJ, 55, 155

Newport News, VA, 37

Niagara Falls, NY, 53

North Dakota, 49

Nyland Co-Housing Community, (Boulder, CO), 75

Oakland, CA, 91, 133

Oceanside, CA, 147

Ohio, 124

Old Town Square (Chicago), 118

Orange County, Florida, 112, 147, 149

Oregon, 147

Orlando, 147, 149, 156

Osborne, David, 59

Oyaski, Mayor Paul, 124

Paradise Valley, AZ, 144

Patton, Dr. Carl V., 57, 58

Pawlukiewicz, Michael, 105, 144

Payne, Billy, 23

Peirce, Neal, 16, 24, 39, 46, 56, 109, 110, 120

Philadelphia, 1, 32, 43, 71, 99, 110, 115, 123, 155-157

Phoenix, 38, 85, 109, 134, 157

Pilla, Bishop Anthony, 23

Pine Avenue Business Association (Niagara Falls, NY), 53

Pioneer Place (Portland, OR), 122

Pittsburgh, 2, 40, 51, 56, 117, 157

Plater-Zyberk, Elizabeth, 151

Port Authority (New York, New Jersey), 14, 63

Porter, Douglas, 100

Portland, OR, 23, 43, 49, 51, 83, 85, 91, 122, 147

Potter, Judge Larry, 104

Power and Light District (Kansas City, MO), 18

Prairie Crossing, IL, 144

Providence, RI, 114

Quality Hill, Kansas City, MO, 145, 146

Rebuild America Coalition, 94

Redmond, WA, 80

Reich, Secretary Robert, 64

Renaissance Center, 118

Rendell, Mayor Edward, 1, 155

Rensselaer, NY, 44

Rhode Island, 147

Richmond, Henry, 98

Richmond, VA, 31-2

Riley, Mayor Joseph, 4, 133

Riverplace, New Haven, CT, 139

Riverside County, CA, 100, 112

Rochester, NY, 99, 110
Rockford, IL, 117
Rohnert Park, CA, 38
Rooney, J. Patrick, 68-9, 72
Rosan, Rick, 42
Rosentraub, Mark, 30
Rouse Company, 122
Rouse, James, 55
Rusk, David, 128
Sacramento, 2, 40, 99, 107, 152
Salt Lake City, UT, 2, 117
San Antonio, 2, 24, 46, 83
San Diego, 24, 90, 136, 137
San Diego County, 111, 112
San Francisco, 40, 56, 127, 138, 91, 156, 157
San Jose, 92
San Ysidro/Otay Mesa, CA, 91
Santa Monica, CA, 15
Sarasota, FL, 63
Saratoga, NY, 44
Schell, Mayor Paul, 31
Schenectady, NY, 44
Schneider, Keith, 99
Schoemehl, Mayor Vincent, Jr., 30
Scottsdale, AZ, 82
Seaside, FL, 151
Seattle, 14, 31, 40, 74, 110, 156, 157
Sedgwick County, KS, 41
Shaker Heights, OH, 124
Shaw Company, The, 80
Shostak, Arthur B., 157
Silicon Valley, 14, 32
Silverman, Robert, 116, 117
Simon Property Group, 122
Somerset Alliance, NJ, 42, 146
South Carolina, 112
South Bend, IN, 128
South Bronx, 119
Spering, Mayor James, 127
Spokane, WA, 30, 37
Spring Island, SC, 112
St. Paul, MN, 133, 149
St. Louis, 29, 30, 32, 44, 56, 57, 85, 88, 110, 123, 146, 152
Staten Island, 14
Stern, Robert A.M., 151

Suisun City, CA, 127
Swaback, Vernon, 82, 134
Taft, Alexander, 111
Talbott, Mayor John, 30, 31
Texas, 129
TIAA-CREF, 122
Tischler & Associates, 110
Toffler, Alvin and Heidi, 11, 32
Trammell Crow Residential, 80
Treasure Valley Institute, 42
TriBeCa (New York City), 70
Trust for Public Land, 53
Tucker, Jack, 131, 132
Turley, Henry, 131, 132
Tuscaloosa, AL, 38
Tuscon, 83
Twin Cities, 43, 47
Tysons Corner, VA, 143
U.S. Conference of Mayors, 46, 103
University City, MO, 123
Unocal Land and Development Company, 112
Upper Darby, PA, 123
Urban Land Institute, 2, 42, 73, 93, 107, 133, 137, 141, 143, 144, 148
Utah, 42
Valley Citizens League in Phoenix, 45
Vancouver, 63
Virginia, 45, 47
Virginia Beach, 15
Vonier, Thomas, 64
Wallis, Allan, 43
Wasatch Front, 42
Washington, DC, 14, 40, 71, 74, 85, 114, 120, 130, 134, 143, 150, 155, 157
West, Cornel, 25
White, Mayor Michael, 23
Whitman, Governor Christine Todd, 146
Whyte, William, 153
Wichita, KS, 41
Williamsburg, 64
Wilmington (Delaware) Area Planning Council, 111
Wisconsin, 103
Woodlands, TX, 112
Yonkers, NY, 117